Responsa in a Moment

Halakhic Responses to Contemporary Issues

David Golinkin

The Institute of Applied Halakhah
at the Schechter Institute of Jewish Studies

Jerusalem 2000

The Meyer and Tirzah Goldstein Holocaust Memorial Library, No. 3

ISBN 965-7105-09-9

Distribution:
The Institute of Applied Halakhah
at the Schechter Institute of Jewish Studies
POB 8600, Jerusalem 91083 Israel

Tel. 02-6790755
Fax 02-6790840
Email: schechter@schechter.org.il

Produced by Leshon Limudim Ltd., Jerusalem
Tel. 02-5372212

Printed in Israel

This third publication of the

Meyer and Tirzah Goldstein Holocaust Memorial Library

is dedicated by

Rabbi Baruch G. Goldstein
"A brand plucked from the fire"

to the memory of the holy and pure martyrs
who perished in the Holocaust

his father *Yisrael Meyer ben Shmuel Alter and Esther Tova Dvorah*
his mother *Tirzah Beila bat Chayyim and Malkah*
his sister *Rachel bat Yisrael Meyer and Tirzah Beila*
his brother *Shmuel Alter ben Yisrael Meyer and Tirzah Beila*

G O L D S T E I N

May their souls be bound up in the bond of everlasting life.

PUBLICATIONS OF THE INSTITUTE OF APPLIED HALAKHAH

David Golinkin, ed., *Proceedings of the Committee on Jewish Law and Standards of the Conservative Movement 1927-1970*, Jerusalem, 1997 (co-published by The Rabbinical Assembly)

David Golinkin, ed., *Responsa of the Va'ad Halakhah of the Rabbinical Assembly of Israel*, Volume 6 (5755-5788) (Hebrew)

THE MEYER AND TIRZAH GOLDSTEIN HOLOCAUST MEMORIAL LIBRARY

No. 1 David Golinkin, *Halakhah for Our Time: The Approach of the Masorti Movement to Halakhah*, Jerusalem, 5758 (Hebrew)

No. 2 David Golinkin, *Halakhah for Our Time: A Conservative Approach to Jewish Law*, Jerusalem, 5758 (Russian)

No. 3 David Golinkin, *Responsa in a Moment*, Jerusalem, 5760

THE RABBI ISRAEL LEVINTHAL CENTER FOR CONTEMPORARY RESPONSA

No. 1 Shmuel Glick, *Education in Light of Israeli Law and Halakhic Literature*, Volume 1, Jerusalem, 5759 (Hebrew)

No. 2 Shmuel Glick, *Education in Light of Israeli Law and Halakhic Literature*, Volume 2, Jerusalem, 5760 (Hebrew)

THE CENTER FOR WOMEN IN JEWISH LAW

David Golinkin, ed., *Jewish Law Watch: The Agunah Dilemma*, Case Study Number One, January 2000 (Hebrew and English)

David Golinkin, ed., *Jewish Law Watch: The Agunah Dilemma*, Case Study Number Two, September 2000 (Hebrew and English)

BOOKS IN PREPARATION

Samuel Dresner and David Golinkin, *Kashrut: A Guide to its Observance and its Meaning for Our Time* (Hebrew)

Shmuel Glick, ed., *Kuntress Hateshuvot: A Bibliography of the Responsa Literature from the Geonic Period until Today* (Hebrew)

David Golinkin, *Women in the Synagogue: A Halakhic Appoach to Change*

David Golinkin, ed., *Halakhic Solutions to the Agunah Dilemma* (Hebrew)

David Golinkin, ed., *Responsa and Halakhic Studies* by Rabbi Isaac Klein, second augmented edition

David Golinkin, ed., *Responsa of the Va'ad Halakhah of the Rabbinical Assembly of Israel*, Volume 7 (Hebrew)

Mikhael Kovsun, translator, *An Anthology of Masorti Responsa* (Russian)

Yossi Turner, ed., *Halakhot Olam: Responsa on Contemporary Halakhic Problems* by Rabbi Hayyim Hirschenson (Hebrew)

David Zohar, ed., *Malki Bakodesh*, Volumes 1-2 by Rabbi Hayyim Hirschenson, second edition (Hebrew)

TABLE OF CONTENTS

INTRODUCTION

In January 1990, I served as Scholar-in-Residence at Congregation Bnai Shalom in Olney, Maryland. That weekend, a Jewish journalist published a sarcastic review of two volumes of the Steinsaltz translation of the Babylonian Talmud in *The Washington Post Magazine* (January 28, 1990, p. 7) which claimed that the Steinsaltz translation of the Talmud was totally irrelevant to modern ethical and legal dilemmas. My friend Niel Meiselman and my father Rabbi Noah Golinkin urged me to write a reply, which was subsequently published on the op-ed page of *The Washington Post* (February 17, 1990, p. A29). In my reply, I explained that Jewish law has been constantly updated since talmudic times through commentaries to the talmud, codes of Jewish law and the responsa literature, in which rabbis have answered over 300,000 individual questions. I then proceeded to answer some of the ethical questions posed by the reviewer.

Hershel Shanks, the Editor of *Moment* magazine, read my article and asked me if I would like to write a column in *Moment* entitled "Responsa", which would show the way Jewish law grapples with modern ethical and legal dilemmas. I readily assented and the column appeared in *Moment* magazine a few times a year between 1990-1996. Some of the questions were asked by the editors of *Moment*, some were questions that I had answered within the framework of the *Va'ad Halakhah* (Law Committee) of the Rabbinical Assembly of Israel, and one was asked by a reader of *Moment*.

Over the years, I have received many favorable comments about the responsa published in *Moment* and a number of people have suggested that I reprint the columns in book form in order to give them some permanence. The result is the present volume, which is organized in the traditional fashion, according to the order of the *Shulhan Arukh*. The responsa which appeared in *Moment* were frequently abbreviated due to lack of space. In this volume I have reprinted the responsa as written and updated some of the bibliography. I have also added a chapter called "The Whys and Hows of Conservative *Halakhah*" in which I try to explain briefly why Conservative Jews observe Jewish law and how Conservative *halakhah* differs from Orthodox *halakhah* using examples from the responsa in this book. It should be noted that the references to *Newsweek* in the footnotes refer to the European edition of that magazine. Reference was made to English bibliography wherever possible, for the benefit of readers not fluent in Hebrew. A glossary of Hebrew terms has been added at the end of the volume for the same reason.

I would like to thank Hershel Shanks and Suzanne Singer, the Editors of *Moment,* who gave me the opportunity to write this innovative column and for their permission to reprint these columns here. I would also like to thank Donny Finkel and his staff at Leshon Limudim who, as usual, produced the book with efficiency and good cheer. This book was edited during a brief sabbatical spent at the Shalom Hartman Institute in Jerusalem; my thanks to Prof. David Hartman and his staff for their warm hospitality. Finally, I would like to thank my uncle, Rabbi Baruch Gershon Goldstein, who had the foresight to establish the Meyer and Tirzah Goldstein Holocaust Memorial Library within our Institute of Applied Halakhah in order to ensure steady publication of books presenting the Conservative/Masorti approach to Jewish law. It is my hope and prayer that this book will encourage Jews, regardless of their background and current level of observance, to study the responsa literature and to allow our tradition to guide them when confronted by modern legal and ethical dilemmas.

David Golinkin
Schechter Institute of Jewish Studies
Jerusalem
13 Sivan 5760

THE WHYS AND HOWS OF CONSERVATIVE HALAKHAH

For the past twenty years I have devoted much of my time to studying and teaching *halakhah* and to writing responsa for Conservative/Masorti Jews. What follows is not the official position of the Conservative or Masorti Movement, but rather the observations of a participant/observer in the making of Conservative *halakhah*.[1]

Both Orthodox and Conservative Judaism are committed to the observance of *halakhah*. They share the belief that to be a good Jew one has to undertake to observe the entire *system* of *halakhah*. This is in keeping with the biblical attitude of "*na'aseh v'nishmah*" ["we shall do and we shall listen"] (Exodus 24:7) and with the rabbinic injunction that "the chief thing is not to expound the law but to do it" (*Avot* 1:17). Both groups would agree with the words of Prof. Louis Ginzberg, one of the leading talmudists and halakhic authorities in the Conservative movement for almost half a century: "*Halakhah* or law is far more fundamental in Judaism than *aggadah* or beliefs, for ideas are volatile but practices endure. If Jewish practice goes, virtually nothing remains".[2]

Nonetheless, there are many differences between the Orthodox and Conservative approaches to *halakhah*. In order to understand the differences, we must address two basic questions: "*Why* observe *halakhah*?" and "*How* do rabbis interpret *halakhah*?".

The "Whys" of Conservative *Halakhah*

The standard Orthodox approach to "why observe *halakhah*" is quite simple: We must observe the commandments because they are Divine in origin; they were given to us in the Torah at Mount Sinai by God himself. A statement by Rabbi Immanuel Jakobovits, late Chief Rabbi of Great Britian, is typical of this approach:

> To me the belief in *Torah min ha-shamayim* (the divine revelation of the Torah) . . . represents a definition of the essence of Judaism as inalienable as the postulate of monotheism ...*Torah min ha-shamayim* essentially means that the Pentateuch as we have it today, is identical with the Torah revealed to Moses at Mount Sinai and that this expression of God's will is authentic, final, and eternally binding upon the Jewish people...[3]

And what about all the laws that were added by the rabbis throughout the ages? According to the fundamentalist approach, they too were given at Mount Sinai as we read in the Palestinian Talmud (*Yerushalmi Peah* 17a and *Yerushalmi Megilah* 74d): "Even what a sharp pupil will expound before his teacher has already been given to Moses at Sinai". In other words, every *mitzvah* we perform as Jews was given *innately* at Mount Sinai. When a rabbi expounds a new law or practice, he is simply revealing something that was hidden in the Torah from the start.

However, this simple or simplistic approach is not satisfying to most Conservative Jews. Many do not believe in a verbal revelation at Mount Sinai. They are troubled by three main problems:

a) In regard to the *act* of revelation, they ask: What happened at Sinai? How do we know that it was God speaking? Perhaps the whole account of the revelation at Sinai is simply a product of someone's imagination. Even if God did speak, how do we know that He was understood correctly?

b) In regard to the *product* of the act of revelation - that is, the Torah - they ask: Is this the direct transcription of God's words? If so, how do we explain some of the contradictions in its laws? For example, Passover is to be celebrated for seven days according to Exodus 13:6, Leviticus 23:6, and Deuteronomy 16:3, but for only six days according to Deuteronomy 16:8. Exodus 20:21 permits the erection of a sanctuary anywhere, but Deuteronomy 12:4-5 restricts the sanctuary to one single shrine in all of Israel. And what about the variations in its stories, such as the different orders of

Creation depicted in Chapters One and Two of Genesis? And how do we explain the similarity of some of its laws (e.g. an eye for an eye) and stories (e.g. the flood stories) to those of the nations surrounding the Israelites during biblical times?

And what about the variant versions of the Bible that we have? Even if God revealed His will at Sinai, human beings have copied it and interpreted it throughout the generations, so how can we be assured that what we have in hand is anything like what God gave, and how do we know that our interpretation of it is anything like what He intended?[4]

c) Finally, the Torah contains laws and stories which raise grave ethical problems. Deuteronomy 23:3 says that a child conceived by his mother from one man while she is still married to another is a *mamzer* who may not marry a Jew "unto the tenth generation". Is it ethical to punish the child and grandchild for the sin of the parents? In Numbers 31, God instructs Moses to take vengeance on the Midianites for the sin of *Ba'al Pe'or* (Numbers 25). When the Israelites return after having killed only the males, Moses is angry at them and instructs them to kill all the remaining Midianites except for young girls. Are these two problematic passages the will of God?

As a result of these problems, many Conservative rabbis and thinkers do not subscribe to the fudamentalist view presented above. They observe *halakhah,* rather, for a combination of reasons, including many of those we shall innumerate below.

1. The first non-fundamentalist approach says that the *halakhah* is the way that the Jewish people throughout the generations *understood* God's revelation at Mount Sinai and interpreted it. A Jew who observes *mitzvot* fulfills God's will as *klal yisrael* - the collective people of Israel - have understood His will for 3,000 years. The most famous advocate of this point of view was Prof. Solomon Schechter, the founder of the Conservative movement. "It is not the mere revealed Bible that is of first importance to the Jew, but the Bible as it repeats itself in history, in other words, as it is interpreted by

Tradition..." The center of authority is removed from the Bible and placed in the hands of the collective conscience of "Catholic Israel" or *klal yisrael*.[5]

2. The second theocentric approach to observance also stresses the partnership of God and man. The Torah and the *mitzvot* express the eternal *brit* or covenant made between God and the Jewish people. As Moses states at the beginning of Deuteronomy (5:3-4): "It was not with our fathers that the Lord made this covenant, but with us, the living, every one of us who is here today. Face to face the Lord spoke to you on the mountain out of the fire". This statement would not be surprising if it had been made to the people who had been present at Mt. Sinai. But Moses is speaking here to their children, forty years later, and yet he says "us", "every one of us", "you"! His point was that the covenant was not a one-shot deal; it is renewed in every generation as Moses clearly explains at the end of Deuteronomy (29:13-14): "I make this convenant not with you alone, but both with those who are standing here with us this day before the Lord our God and with those who are not with us here this day". And Rashi, the classic medieval commentator, adds: "And with future generations as well". Every time we observe a commandment or *halakhah*, we thereby renew our convenant with God.

3. The third God-centered approach states that *mitzvot* lead us to holiness, they sanctify our lives, and bring us closer to God. This was the approach taught by the Tanna Issi ben Yehuda in the *Mekhilta* (*Parasha* 20, ed. Horovitz-Rabin, p. 320) 1800 years ago: "With each new command, God adds holiness to the people of Israel". This approach is also reflected in the standard formula of blessings recited over *mitzvot* such as Shabbat and Chanukah candles, *lulav, tefilin* and *tallit*: *"asher kidshanu b'mitzvotav v'tzivanu"*, "Blessed are You O Lord our God King of the Universe *who has sanctified us* with his *mitzvot* and commanded us...". And indeed, the *mitzvot* do sanctify our lives - the mundane becomes special and the profane becomes holy. Shabbat and festivals sanctify time. Blessings and *kashrut* sanctify our meals. The wedding ceremony and the laws

of *mikveh* sanctify marriage. The laws of *ona'ah* (overcharging) and *eifat tzedek* (accurate weights and measures) sanctify business. Thus, through the observance of *mitzvot,* we strive to fulfill the verse found in Exodus (19:6): "And you shall be unto Me a kingdom of Priests and a holy nation" as well as the verse found in Leviticus (19:2): "You shall be holy for I, the Lord Your God, am Holy."

The next three reasons are ethnocentric. They posit that the *mitzvot* serve to preserve, unite, and strengthen the Jewish people.

1. According to the first approach, the *halakhah* is the "cement" which binds together the scattered "bricks" of the Jewish people. Without this cement, the Jewish people would have long ago disintegrated. The *mitzvot* tie every Jew in the world to every other Jew in the world. In the past few years, I have prayed in synagogues from Los Angeles to Milwaukee to New York, from Haifa to Eilat, and from London to Rome and I have always been struck by the fact that 95% of the services are identical, no matter where you go. Similarly, when I put on *tefilin* every morning, I know that a Jew in Morocco does the same. When I light candles on Chanukah, I know that a Jew in Argentina does the same. When I give *tzedakah,* I know that a Jew in Australia does the same. Thus the commandments help us fulfill the prayer we recite every Shabbat in the *Minchah* service: "Who is like your people Israel, one united nation in the world!".

2. The second people-centered approach stresses the historical continuity of the Jewish people. The *mitzvot* are the golden chain which binds us and our children to our ancestors and the history of our people. Without them we would lose our continuity and we would feel like orphans in history. When I observe Shabbat, I know that Moses did the same and when I wear *tefilin,* I know that Rabbi Akiva did the same. When I give *tzedakah,* I know that Maimonides did the same and when I study Torah, I know that the Gaon of Vilna did the same. Jews who observe *halakhah* are plugged in to the history and traditions of their people.

3. The third ethnocentric approach is extremely pragmatic. The greatest threat to the survival of the Jewish people today is assimilation and intermarriage. For thousands of years the *mitzvot*

have protected the Jewish people from these threats and ensured Jewish continuity. The famous Zionist thinker Ahad Ha'am said: "more than the Jewish people has preserved the Sabbath, the Sabbath has preserved the Jews". The same can be said of all the *mitzvot*. Observant Jews do not put Christmas trees in their houses, they do not experiment with cults and drugs, and their children, for the most part, do not marry non-Jews. Therefore, the *halakhah* is an excellent bulwark against assimilation.

The last two reasons I shall outline, are anthropocentric or man-centered. They maintain that each individual performs the *mitzvot* primarily for the personal benefits he or she derives from them.

1. The first such approach views the *mitzvot* as a means of self-discipline, to improve our characters, and to make us better human beings. This idea sounds very modern, but it is not. It was originally emphasized by the Amora Rav who lived in Babylon in the third century. He said: "The commandments were only given in order to refine and discipline the person who performs them" (*Genesis Rabbah* 44:1, ed. Theodor-Albeck, pp. 424-425). Abraham ibn Ezra of twelfth-century Spain concurred. In his classic commentary to the Torah he states (Deut. 5:18): "The main purpose of all the commandments is to straighten the heart". Since heart in Hebrew is frequently synonymous with mind, Ibn Ezra means that the main purpose of all the commandments is to refine and discipline the mind.

This idea was reiterated in our time by Rabbi Harold Kushner, a Conservative Rabbi who lives in Massachusetts:

> So many of the rules and rituals of the Jewish way of life are spiritual calisthenics, designed to teach us to control the most basic instincts of our lives - hunger, sex, anger, acquisitiveness and so on. We are not directed to deny or stifle them, but to control them, to rule them rather than let them rule us...The freedom the Torah offers us is the freedom to say no to our appetites.[6]

2. The second and last approach states very simply: Perform *mitzvot* because they are fun! They uplift the spirit and bring joy to the heart.

This point of view has been popular from the Bible until today. The Psalmist wrote (19:9) three thousand years ago: "The precepts of the Lord are just, making the heart rejoice".

The rabbis of the Talmud developed this idea into the concept of "*simhah shel mitzvah*", the joy of performing a *mitzvah*. Time after time in rabbinic literature we are told that one should perform the commandments with joy. We learn, for example, in the tractate of *Berakhot* (31a): "One does not stand up to recite the *Amidah*, unless he does so out of the joy of performing a *mitzvah*".

When it comes right down to it, many Jews perform many *mitzvot* because they enjoy them. I observe Shabbat because I enjoy observing Shabbat; it is the one day of the week when I can really relax and spend time with my family. When we stay up learning all night at a *tikkun* every Shavuot, we do so because it is fun! And why do we dance like maniacs on Simchat Torah and dress up like clowns on Purim? Because it is fun! And why do we build a Sukkah and eat there for seven days? Because it is fun! Jewish law is not a burden; it is a joy, "*simhah shel mitzvah*" – the joy of performing a *mitzvah*.

In summation, the "why" of Conservative *halakhah* is more complex than the "why" of Orthodox *halakhah*. Orthodox Jews observe Jewish law because they view all or much of it as the literal will of God. Conservative Jews observe *halakhah* for a variety of different reasons. Orthodox fundamentalism frequently leads to rigid interpretations of Jewish law, while Conservative non-fundamentalism frequently leads to more liberal interpretations, as we shall see below.

The "Hows" of Conservative *Halakhah*

The Conservative movement does not have one uniform set of principles guiding the rabbis who make halakhic decisions and, indeed, there are diverse approaches among Conservative halakhic authorities. However, close study of the responsa or halakhic decisions written by Conservative rabbis during the past ninety years reveals six general characteristics of Conservative *halakhah*, five of which frequently distinguish Conservative responsa from Orthodox responsa. In this section, we shall outline each general characteristic and illustrate it using the responsa found in this volume.

1. One of the mottos of the Conservative Movement is "tradition and change". Changes are not made for the sake of change, but only in order to deal with an urgent or acute problem. Frequently, after examining all sides of a halakhic issue, Conservative rabbis simply favor the tradition over any change. Thus, for example, my responsum on avoiding charity cheaters (pp. 51-56) is based on the opinion of Rav Yehudah (*Bava Batra* 9a) as codified in the standard codes of Jewish law. He said that one investigates when someone asks for clothing, but not when asked for food. I derived from this that one waives investigation when faced with an urgent situation of human suffering, but should investigate unknown or new charities before giving them *tzedakah*. In other words, my answer was based primarily on the traditional approach to this question with some adjustment to modern situations.

2. Frequently, a rabbi has many different halakhic options from which to choose and he or she can rule strictly or leniently or somewhere in the middle. Conservative rabbis usually prefer a lenient ruling to a strict one. This is based on the talmudic teaching " 'You shall keep My statutes and My laws which if a man shall do he shall *live* by them' (Leviticus 18:5) - and not *die* because of them" (*Yoma* 85b) and on the talmudic dictum "the strength of a lenient ruling is greater" (*Berakhot* 60a).

Thus, for example, in my responsum on whether Israel should return territory captured in 1967 for the sake of peace (pp. 31-36), I compared the strict attitude favored by the followers of Rabbi Zvi Yehudah Kuk z"l and *Gush Emunim* to the lenient attitude of Rabbi Ovadia Yosef and Rabbi Theodore Friedman z"l. After examining both sides of the issue, I sided with the latter group and ruled that it is permissible to return territories for the sake of peace.

3. One of the greatest differences between Conservative and Orthodox rabbis is their attitude towards modern sciences and

methods of study such as history, archaeology, text criticism and medicine. Many Orthodox responsa are totally unaware of or actively opposed to these disciplines, and even if they do cite medical studies, it is almost never with an exact reference to medical literature. Conservative rabbis feel that not only is it *permissible* to utilize modern methods and knowledge to write responsa; it is *essential* to do so because you cannot arrive at a correct halakhic decision until you know and understand the facts.

Thus, almost all Conservative responsa contain a historical-chronological survey of the topic in order to determine if it derives from the Torah, the talmud, the early rabbis or the later rabbis. There is more readiness to change a relatively new *halakhah* or one which was not adopted by the entire community or something which is only a custom. They also utilize other modern sciences and methodologies. My responsum on *shucklen* [swaying] during study and prayer (pp. 25-28) quotes both Mohammed and the Moslem poet Labid as quoted by Ignaz Goldziher in a German article published in 1871. My responsum on the *kashrut* of veal raised on factory farms (pp. 73-77) opens with a description of calf-husbandry based on the books *Calf Husbandry, Health and Welfare* and *The Calf.* My responsa on medical issues such as telling the truth to terminal patients (pp. 57-63), genetic engineering (pp. 67-72) and smoking (pp. 93-98) were only written after reading medical journals such as *Nature, Science, The Journal of Medicine and Philosophy,* and *Journal of the American Medical Association.*

4. The *Shulhan Arukh* written in the sixteenth century by Rabbi Yosef Karo along with the Ashkenazic glosses of Rabbi Moshe Isserles is one of the standard codes of Jewish law. However, it has attained almost canonical status among Orthodox rabbis. Conservative rabbis have great respect for the *Shulhan Arukh,* but do not view it as the ultimate authority because it was written over 400 years ago and much has changed since then in the *halakhah,* in society and in our outlook on life. In addition, when the *Shulhan Arukh* was published, many important halakhic authorities severely criticized those who decided Jewish law according to the *Shulhan Arukh*

without checking the Talmud and the major authorites who preceded Rabbi Yosef Karo.

Thus, in a Hebrew responsum published elsewhere, I was asked whether it is permissible to move a Torah scroll for a one-time reading such as at a retreat or in the house of a mourner. Rabbi Yosef Karo ruled in two different places in the *Shulhan Arukh* that one may not bring a Torah scroll to Jewish prisoners even on the High Holidays. Many Orthodox rabbis would simply stop there; I did not. I discovered that Rabbi Yosef Karo's ruling is based on a responsum by Rabbi Meir of Rothenburg which is based in turn on a passage in the Palestinian Talmud which says that one may only move a Torah scroll for a one-time reading for an important person such as a High Priest or an Exilarch. However, according to the *Mishnah* and the Babylonian Talmud, it is generally permissible to move a Torah scroll for a one-time reading. Normally, when there is a dispute between the Palestinian and Babylonian talmuds, we follow the latter. Furthermore, the strict approach was the exception to the rule. Most authorities permitted bringing a Torah scroll to a sick and/or important person or to the house of a mourner or to the house of a groom or for the sake of a group of people.[7]

5. The Conservative movement believes in halakhic pluralism. Not all halakhic questions have one simple answer; sometimes, there are two or more legitimate ways of ruling on a given halakhic issue. My responsum on institutionalizing parents with Alzheimer's disease (pp. 37-42) presents children facing this dilemma with three legitimate halakhic options. My responsum on telling the truth to terminal patients (pp. 57-63) maintains that most patients should be told the truth because they want to know the truth, but makes allowance for the minority of patients who do not wish to know the truth. My responsum on *shucklen* (pp. 25-28) presents seven different reasons for this custom without claiming that only one of them is the correct answer.

6. Finally, Conservative rabbis place great emphasis on the moral component of Judaism and the *halakhah*. The *mitzvot* between man and man are no less important than those between man and God.

"Keep far from falsehood" (Exodus 23:7) is no less important than "Remember the Sabbath day to keep it holy" (ibid. 20:8). Paying taxes is no less important than sitting in the Sukkah. Honoring one's parents is no less important than keeping kosher.

That is why six of the twelve responsa in this collection deal with moral and ethical dilemmas. Our attitude towards parents with Alzheimer's disease (pp. 37-42) is just as important as our attitude towards Torah study (pp. 43-49). Our attitude towards charity cheaters (pp. 51-56) is just as important as our attitude towards making *aliyah* (pp. 79-83).

In conclusion, Conservative Judaism is sometimes depicted by its opponents as a wishy-washy stream in Judaism somewhere between Orthodoxy and Reform without a clear ideology. It is obvious from the above that Conservative Judaism is halakhically distinct from Orthodoxy and Reform. Unlike the Reform movement, it views the *halakhah* as binding on all Jews. But, as we have seen, it differs from Orthodoxy both in the whys and hows of its *halakhah*.

NOTES

1. This chapter is based on my booklet *Halakhah for Our Time: A Conservative Approach to Jewish Law*, New York, 1991, pp. 9-16, 29-32.
2. Quoted in Seymour Siegel, ed., *Conservative Judaism and Jewish Law*, New York, 1977, p. 51. Regarding Prof. Ginzberg's contributions to Conservative *halakhah*, see David Golinkin, ed., *The Responsa of Professor Louis Ginzberg*, Jerusalem and New York, 1996.
3. *The Condition of Jewish Belief*, Northvale, New Jersey, 1995, pp. 109-110.
4. Elliot Dorff, *Conservative Judaism: Our Ancestors to Our Descendants*, New York, 1977, pp. 111-112.
5. Solomon Schechter, *Studies in Judaism*, First Series, London, 1896, pp. xvii-xviii.
6. Harold Kushner, *To Life*, Boston, Toronto, London, 1993, pp. 51-52.
7. David Golinkin in idem., ed., *Responsa of the Va'ad Halakhah of the Rabbinical Assembly of Israel*, Volume 6 (5755-5758), pp. 81-90 (Hebrew).

RESPONSA RELATED TO ORAH HAYYIM

WHY DO JEWS SWAY WHEN THEY PRAY?

OH 48 in *Rema*

Question: *Why do Jews sway when they pray?*

Responsum: Like many Jewish customs, the origins of *shucklen* – a common Yiddish word which means to shake or rock – are shrouded in mystery.[1] We can say when it was done and where but not why. This is because many customs were instituted by the Jewish people as a spontaneous expresion of their Jewishness; the learned explanations came later.

Shucklen is not explicitly mentioned in the Talmud.[2] Interestingly enough, it is first mentioned in a number of Islamic sources. Mohammed is supposed to have said: "Be not like the Jews who whenever they read the Torah publicly move to and fro". His contemporary, the poet Labid (d. 660), writes of a person who gropes for an object, moving his hand to and fro "like a praying Jew".[3]

Jewish sources also mention *shucklen* in the context of Torah study and prayer. Rabbi Samuel Hanaggid of Granada (d. 1056) is the first to mention swaying during Torah study in one of his poems:

> And we came angry into the House of God
> and would that we had taken a wrong turn,
> for behold the rabbi and the students were swaying
> their heads like a tamarisk in the wilderness.[4]

Various reasons have been given for this practice throughout the ages.

Rabbi Judah Halevi of Spain (d. 1141) gives two explanations in his book, *The Kuzari*, an imaginary dialogue between the king of the

Khazars and a rabbi. The king asks why Jews move to and fro when they read the Bible. The rabbi replies:

> It is said that it is done in order to arouse natural heat [i.e., to warm up]. My personal belief [is as follows:]... As it often happened that many persons read at the same time, it was possible that ten or more read from one volume. Each of them was obliged to bend down in his turn in order to read a passage, and to turn back again. This resulted in a continual bending and sitting up, the book lying on the ground. This was one reason. Then it became a habit through constant seeing, observing and imitating, which is in man's nature. [5]

Rabbi Simhah of Vitry (France, d. 1105) gives a third explanation. He says that young children are taught to sway when they study the Torah, "for thus we find at the giving of the Torah 'And the people saw and they trembled' (Exodus 20:15)".[6]

Lastly, the Zohar, which was written in thirteenth-century Spain, asks:

> Why is it that all the peoples of the world do not sway, but Jews alone do so when they study Torah? The souls of Israel are derived from the Holy Lamp [of God] ...when a Jew utters one word of Torah, the light [in his soul] is kindled...and he sways to and fro like the flame of a candle.[7]

On the other hand, there was a common custom of swaying during prayer. This custom was explained in at least three different ways.

Rabbi Abraham of Lunel (Toledo, d. 1215) and many others quote an unknown midrash:

> A person is required to sway during prayer, as it is written: "all my bones shall proclaim: O God, who is like You!" (Psalms 35:10)...And this is the custom of the Rabbis of France and her pious ones.[8]

The testament attributed to R. Israel Ba'al Shem Tov (d. 1760) gives a different explanation for *shucklen*:

> When a person is drowning in a river and he makes

> movements in order to extricate himself from the water, those who see him will no doubt laugh at him and at his motions. Thus, when a person prays and makes motions, one should not laugh at him because he is saving himself from the malicious waters which are the... foreign thoughts which come to distract him during prayer.[9]

In other words, *shucklen* helps one concentrate on the prayers and say them with *kavanah* [proper intent].

Lastly, two nineteenth-century authors came up with a truly original explanation for *shucklen*: Jewish students and rabbis don't get enough exercise. Therefore, they shuckle when they study and pray in order to get some badly needed exercise![10]

Surprisingly, a number of prominent rabbis opposed *shucklen* during prayer. They claimed that it was disrespectful[11] or that it prevents the proper *kavanah* required for the *Amidah* [the silent devotion].[12]

In conclusion, Jews have shuckled during prayer and study for at least 1,400 years. While the original reason is not known, most Jews seem to feel that it helps one concentrate during prayer and study. On the other hand, there is certainly no obligation to shuckle. The best rule of thumb is probably that stated by R. Yehiel Michal Epstein (d. 1908):

> And during the *Amidah* there are some who sway and some who don't and it depends on the person's nature. If by swaying, his *kavanah* improves, then he should sway; and a person whose *kavanah* is clearer when he stands perfectly still should not sway — and [either option] should be done for the sake of heaven...[13]

NOTES

1. There is a vast literature about *shucklen*. In English, see *The Jewish Encyclopedia*, Vol. 11, New York, 1905, p. 607. In Hebrew, see Senior Sachs, *Hamizpah* 1/4 (1885), pp. 9-12 and the thorough discussion by Yitzhak Zimmer, who quotes over fifty sources, in *Sidra* 5 (1989), pp. 116-127 = idem., *Olam K'minhago Noheig*, Jerusalem, 1996, pp. 97-108.
2. It may be hinted at in *Eruvin* 53b-54a and *Shabbat* 104a.

3. For these and other Arabic sources see Ignaz Goldziher, *MGWJ* 20 (1871), pp. 178-183 (in German).
4. Dov Yarden, ed., *The Diwan of R. Samuel Hanagid,* Jerusalem, 1966, p. 229.
5. The *Kuzari,* translated by H. Hirschfeld, New York, 1964, p. 128. Regarding the scarcity of Hebrew books in the Middle Ages, see my article in *Kiryat Sefer* 62 (5748-5749), pp. 435-436.
6. S. Hurwitz, ed., *Mahzor Vitry,* Berlin, 1893, pp. 628, 630. This explanation is repeated in many later sources.
7. *Zohar* to Numbers, fols. 218b-219a.
8. Yitzhak Refael, ed., *Sefer Hamanhig,* Jerusalem, 1978, p. 85.
9. Quoted by Zimmer, *Sidra,* p. 124.
10. Dr. Shimon Brainin, *Orah Lahayyim,* Vilna, 1883, p. 126 and R. Haim Aryeh Leib Fenster, *Sha'ar Bat Rabbim to* Genesis, New York, 1953, fol. 7b.
11. R. Jacob Anatoli (d. 1256), *Malmad Hatalmidim,* Lyck, 1866, fol. 159a.
12. R. Menahem Azariah of Fano (d. 1620), R. Menahem de Lonzano (d. 1624) and R. Isaiah Horwitz (d. 1630) among others — see Zimmer, *Sidra,* pp. 121-122 and see p. 127 for Sephardic opposition.
13. *Arukh Hashulhan, Orah Hayyim* 48:3.

RESPONSA RELATED TO YOREH DE'AH

RETURNING TERRITORIES FOR THE SAKE OF PEACE

YD 157:1

Question: *Does Jewish law permit the State of Israel to give back all or part of the territories captured in 1967 for the sake of peace?*

Responsum: This is an extremely complex and emotional issue that has been widely debated by halakhic authorities since the Six-Day War.[1] This is because *Eretz Yisrael* holds such a special place in Jewish tradition and history.[2] Indeed, God's very first conversations with Abraham concern *Eretz Yisrael:*

> Go forth from your native land to the land that I will show you...I will give this land to your offspring (Genesis 12:1,7).

And again:

> Raise your eyes and look out from where you are, to the north and south, to the east and west, for I give you all the land that you see to you and your offspring forever (Genesis 13:14-15).

This promise is reiterated on numerous occasions to Isaac (Genesis 26:1-6), Jacob (Genesis 35:11-12) and Moses (Exodus 6:2-8).

Furthermore, *Eretz Yisrael,* the Promised Land, is inherently holy. According to the Torah, Israel's predecessors were expelled from the land because they defiled the holiness of the land (Leviticus 18:24-28 and Genesis 15:16). According to the rabbis, the land of Israel is the holiest of all lands *(Mishnah Kelim* 1:6). Prophecy only takes place in the land of Israel or regarding the land of Israel.[3] *Eretz Yisrael* is also special because many of the *mitzvot,* such as the Sabbatical year, can only be performed there *(Kiddushin* 36b and *Sota* 14a). The rabbis went so far as to say that whoever lives outside of *Eretz Yisrael* is considered as one who has no God (*Ketubot* 110b) and whoever is buried in *Eretz Yisrael* is considered as if he had been buried under the altar (*Ketubot* 111a).

Now that we have established the Jewish people's deep theological and spiritual ties to *Eretz Yisrael,* we can examine the conflicting halakhic claims regarding territorial compromise.

Those who oppose territorial compromise advance at least three basic arguments. Some declare that it is halakhically forbidden to return any part of *"Eretz Yisrael hashleimah"* ["the complete land of Israel"]. Rabbi Theodore Friedman, however, has conclusively shown that there is no such concept in Jewish tradition because Israel's borders changed countless times throughout Jewish history both in theory and in practice.[4] One example from the biblical period will suffice: God promised Abraham the land "from the *River* of Egypt" (Genesis 15:18), while he promised the Israelites the land from "the *Wadi* of Egypt" (Numbers 34:5). The "River of Egypt" is the Nile, while the "Wadi of Egypt" is Wadi el Arish, which is 180 miles east of the Nile!

Similar flexibility of boundaries is evident in the rabbinic period when the rabbis needed to define the borders of Israel for the purpose of observing *mitzvot* such as tithing and the Sabbatical year. The borders changed from *mitzvah* to *mitzvah* and the main criterion for inclusion seems to have been the Jewish population of the town. Thus Caesarea, a city inhabited by pagans and Jews, was originally considered part of *Eretz Yisrael* for the purpose of tithes and the Sabbatical year, but was later excluded.[5] Similarly, Bet She'an, Bet Guvrin and Kefar Zemah were originally considered part of *Eretz Yisrael* vis-à-vis tithing, but Rabbi Judah the Prince excluded them from *Eretz Yisrael* when the Jewish population shrank.[6] Thus, the borders of *Eretz Yisrael* were fluid and the concept "the complete land of Israel" has no basis in our classical sources.

Others object to handing over territories to non-Jews on the basis of Deuteronomy 7:1-2:

> When the Lord your God brings you to the land that you are about to enter and possess, and He dislodges many nations before you... seven nations much larger than you... you must

> doom them to destruction, grant them no terms and have no mercy upon them (*lo tehonem*).

This is the simple meaning of "*lo tehonem*", but the rabbis explained it to mean "do not give them a hold (*hanayah*) on the land" (*Avodah Zarah* 20a). *Tosafot* (ad. loc.) interpret this to mean that one may not sell or give parts of *Eretz Yisrael* to *any* non-Jew. This approach would rule out any territorial compromise. However, many authorities rule that this prohibition applies only to *idol worshippers* such as the seven nations mentioned in the verse, lest they "turn your children away from me to worship other gods" (Deuteronomy 7:4).[7] Therefore, since Moslems are not idol worshippers, many authorities rule that it is permissible to sell or give them parts of *Eretz Yisrael*[8] and territorial concessions to Arabs would thus be permitted.

Lastly, other opponents of territorial compromise rely on the opinion of Nahmanides. The book of Numbers (33:53) states: "And you shall take possession of the land and settle in it, for I have assigned the land to you to possess". Nahmanides interprets that verse as a positive commandment: "...that we may not leave the land in the hands of other nations. ..and the Sages called this a commanded war".[9] In other words, we are commanded to conquer *Eretz Yisrael* and keep her in Jewish hands regardless of the danger and any loss of Jewish life that might occur in the process. However, some reject Nahmanides' opinion because he is the only one who considers it a *mitzvah* to capture and retain the land of Israel.[10] Others have explained that even according to Nahmanides, this *mitzvah* only applies in the days of the Messiah.[11]

On the other hand, there are at least three arguments in favor of territorial compromise:

Rabbi Ovadiah Yosef, former Sephardic Chief Rabbi of Israel, has emphasized that *pikuah nefesh*, the saving of human life, takes precedence over all the commandments in the Torah except for idol worship, forbidden sexual relationships and murder (*Sanhedrin* 74a). Thus, even if it were a *mitzvah* to keep the territories under Jewish sovereignty, *pikuah nefesh* would take precedence. As Rabbi Yosef states:

> Therefore, if the military commanders along with the members of the cabinet decide that it is an issue of *pikuah nefesh*...that if territories are returned, the threat of war shall be decreased and there is the possibility of lasting peace, it appears that according to all halakhic opinions it is permissible to return territories of *Eretz Yisrael* for the sake of attaining this goal, for nothing stands in the way of *pikuah nefesh*.[12]

Secondly, there is a clear biblical precedent for handing over Israeli territory for the sake of peace:

> Since King Hiram of Tyre had supplied Solomon with all the cedar and cypress timber and gold that he required [for building the Temple], *King Solomon, in turn, gave Hiram twenty towns in the region of Galilee* (I Kings 9:11).[13]

If King Solomon was permitted to give away twenty towns in the Galilee as a token of friendship for services rendered, we too are permitted to give away sections of *Eretz Yisrael* for the sake of peace.

And this leads us to the last point. Peace is one of the great ideals of Judaism: "By three things is the world preserved: by justice, by truth and by peace" *(Avot* 1:18). "If the Jewish people worships idols but lives in peace with each other, God forgives them" *(Sifrei Naso,* par. 42). "Great is peace, for all major prayers and blessings end with the word *Shalom"* (ibid.). But it is not enough to sit back and wait for peace to happen. The Psalmist said: "*Seek* peace and *pursue* it" (Psalm 34:15). "Hillel said: be of the disciples of Aaron, loving peace and *pursuing* peace" *(Avot* 1:12*),* while the parallel passage explains that Aaron used to run back and forth between two antagonists until peace was achieved.[14]

In conclusion, we have here a classic case of conflicting values in Judaism – our love of *Eretz Yisrael* vs. our desire to save human life and our desire to pursue peace. The choice is not an easy one and has justifiably aroused strong emotions on both sides of the issue. Yet, in light of the sources presented above, it seems clear that when the majority of the political and military leaders of the State of Israel decide that giving up certain territories will ultimately save lives and lead to peace, Jewish law permits us – and perhaps even requires us – to do so.

NOTES

1. See J. David Bleich, *Contemporary Halachic Problems*, Vol. II, New York, 1983, pp. 189-221; *Journal of Halacha and Contemporary Society* XVI (Fall 1988) pp. 55-95 and XVIII (Fall 1989), pp. 77-110.
2. For the centrality of *Eretz Yisrael* in Jewish tradition, see Abraham Halkin, ed., *Zion in Jewish Literature*, New York, 1961; Lawrence Hoffman, ed., *The Land of Israel: Jewish Perspectives*, Notre Dame, 1986; and Benjamin Segal, *Returning: The Land of Israel as Focus in Jewish History*, Jerusalem, 1987.
3. *Mekhilta, Pisha*, chapter 1, ed. Lauterbach, vol. 1, pp. 4-8 and especially Judah Halevi, *The Kuzari*, Part Two, paragraphs 13-14, translated by H. Hirschfeld, New York, 1964, pp. 89-92.
4. Rabbi Theodore Friedman, *Responsa of the Va'ad Halakhah of the Rabbinical Assembly of Israel* 2 (5747), pp. 73-77 = David Golinkin, ed., *Be'er Tuviah*, Jerusalem, 1991, Hebrew section, pp. 53-58. For a visual presentation of Israel's shifting borders in ancient times, see Prof. Jacob Milgrom in *Moment*, August 1996, pp. 52-53, 77 and *The Macmillan Bible Atlas*, Revised Third Edition, New York, 1993, maps no. 68, 69, 90, 98, 104-105, 158, 165, 170.
5. *Tosefta Oholot* 18:16-17, ed. Zuckermandel, p. 617 along with a thorough explanation by Lee Levine, *Caesarea Under Roman Rule*, Leiden, 1975, pp. 67-68.
6. *Yerushalmi Demai*, Chapter 2, fol. 22c and *Hullin* 6b and cf. the explanation of Gedaliah Alon, *The Jews in Their Land in the Talmudic Age*, II, Jerusalem, 1984, p. 731.
7. *Tur Hoshen Mishpat* 249 and the *Bah* ad. loc.; *Responsa of the Rashba*, I, no. 8; the Meiri to *Avoda Zarah* 20a.
8. R. Raphael Meyuhass, *Mizbah Adamah*, Salonika, 1777, fol. 12b; R. Abraham Isaac Kuk, *Responsa Mishpat Kohen*, no. 63; R. Zvi Pesach Frank, *Kerem Tziyon*, vol. 3, p. 13; R. Yitzhak Isaac Halevi Herzog, *Shanah B'shanah* 5746, pp. 136-140; R. Shaul Yisraeli, *Amud Hayemini*, no. 12, par. 3; and R. Ovadiah Yosef cited below in note 12.
9. Nahmanides' additions to *Sefer Hamitzvot* by the Rambam, no. 4 and cf. Nahmanides' commentary to the verse.
10. Maimonides, *Sefer Hahinukh* and others do not include it in their enumerations of the 613 *mitzvot*. Cf. below, pp. 79-83, where I accept Nahmanides' approach to *aliyah*, which is based on his view that it's a *mitzvah* to conquer the land. Even so, I am in favor of returning territories for the sake of peace for the reasons explained below.
11. R. Isaac de Leon in *Megilat Esther* to *Sefer Hamitzvot* ad. loc. and others.

12. *Torah Shebe'al Peh* 21 (5740), p. 14 and again ibid., 31 (5750), p. 16. Of course, some say we will save more Jewish lives by not returning the territories, but today most Israeli political and military leaders disagree.
13. The parallel passage in II Chronicles 8:2 says the opposite, but that version seems to be later apologetics – see *Entziklopedia Mikrait*, vol. 4, col. 6. For other explanations, see Radak to both verses as well as Jacob Myers, *The Anchor Bible: II Chronicles*, Garden City, New York, 1965, p. 47.
14. *Avot D'rabi Nattan*, Version B, Chapter 24, ed. Schechter, p. 49 and cf. Version A, Chapter 12, pp. 48-49.

INSTITUTIONALIZING PARENTS WITH ALZHEIMER'S DISEASE

ꕤ YD 240:10 ꕤ

Question: *As life expectancy grows, many people are faced with the difficulties of caring for a parent with Alzheimer's disease.*[1] *According to Jewish law, is it permissible to institutionalize such a parent?*

Responsum: This question presents a difficult moral dilemma. On the one hand, the Torah commands us to "Honor your father and your mother" (Exodus 20:12, Deuteronomy 5:16) and again: "You shall each revere his mother and his father" (Leviticus 19:3), which seem to be absolute requirements regardless of their behavior. On the other hand, if the parent has deteriorated to such an extent that he or she requires being strapped into bed or being drugged or having a diaper changed, is it "honor" and "reverence" for a child to do this? Or is it greater honor for an outsider to do so? What about the emotional strains on the child? How much must he or she bear?

This sounds like a new dilemma but, in fact, the problem of parents who have deteriorated mentally is mentioned in Jewish sources as early as the second century b.c.e., and the specific question raised above has been hotly debated by halakhic authorities for over 800 years.

The apocryphal book of Ben Sira, dating to the second century b.c.e., tells us (3:12-13):

> My son, be strong in the honor of your father; and do not leave him all the days of your life. *Even if he loses sense, let him do [all that he wishes]* and do not shame him all the days of his life.

A post-Talmudic midrash teaches much the same thing:

> Even if your father's spittle is running down his beard, obey him immediately.[2]

The Talmud does not explicitly deal with our issue, but it contains three passages which discuss the erratic behavior of parents.[3] Dama ben Netina, the gentile "Mayor" of first-century Ashkelon, was once chairing a meeting of the City Council. His mother entered, tore off his golden silk cloak, hit him on the head, and spat in his face – but he did nothing to shame her.[4]

Another Talmudic passage reads:

> They asked Rabbi Eliezer: "To what extent must one honor one's father and mother?" He replied: "To the extent that if he takes your wallet and throws it in the sea, you should not shame him" (*Kiddushin* 32a).

These two Talmudic passages were codified by Maimonides (*Mamrim* 6:7) and Rabbi Joseph Karo (*Shulhan Arukh, Yoreh Deah* 240:3, 8) and they seem to agree with *Ben Sira* and *Seder Eliyahu* – no matter what you parent does, you must obey him and not shame him.

But if this is the case, what can a child do if he can no longer bear his parent's strange or abnormal behavior? This dilemma is dealt with in a third Talmudic passage which became the basis for most subsequent halakhic discussion:

> Rav Assi [who lived in Babylon] had an aged mother. She said to him: "I want jewelry!" He made some for her. "I want a husband!" He replied: "I'll look for one for you." "I want a husband as handsome as you!" He left her and went to Israel. When he heard that she was coming after him, he asked Rabbi Yohanan: "Is it permissible to leave Israel for *Hutz La'aretz* [the Diaspora]?" He replied: "It is forbidden." [He asked:] "Towards his mother – what is the law?" He replied: "I don't know."... In the meantime, Rav Assi heard that her coffin was coming. He said: "Had I known, I would not have left Babylon!" [Or: "Had I known, I would not have asked permission to leave Israel!"] (*Kiddushin* 31b).

This story is very problematic. Was Rav Assi's mother mentally disturbed (she seems to be interested in marrying her own son) or merely crotchety? Can a child run away when he can no longer tolerate a parent's erratic behavior? And what does the final ambiguous sentence mean? Did Rav Assi regret abandoning his mother or is he saying that not only did he act properly by leaving her, but he was not even required to meet her coffin?

The halakhic authorities interpreted this story in two conflicting directions. Maimonides (1135-1204) and his followers used it to legitimate custodial care, while Ra'avad of Posquieres (1120-1198) and his followers came to the opposite conclusion.

Maimonides codified the story as follows:

> If one's father or mother should become mentally disordered, he should try to treat them as their mental state demands, until God has pity on them. But if he finds he cannot endure the situation because of their extreme madness, let him leave them and go away, *commanding others to care for them* as *befits them (Mamrim* 6:10).

According to the last sentence, it is perfectly legitimate to institutionalize a parent with Alzheimer's disease, even though this is not explicitly stated in the story about Rav Assi.

Ra'avad of Posquieres (1120-1198), Maimonides' classic critic, disagrees (*Hassagot,* ad. loc.):

> This is not a correct ruling! If he goes and leaves him, *who* shall he command to watch him?!

Apparently, in Ra'avad's time and place there was no option of custodial care and, indeed, the first Jewish old age home seems to have been founded in Amsterdam in 1749.[5]

All subsequent halakhic authorities aligned themselves with either Maimonides or Ra'avad. The Maimonidean camp,[6] replies that since Rav Assi's mother was brought to Israel in a coffin, he must have ordered others to take care of his mother. Regarding the practical issue raised by Ra'avad, they reply that the child can hire someone to take care of the parent. They further state that in cases of a parent who has deteriorated mentally, an outsider can do a better job than a child for two reasons: First of all, the parent will be embarrassed to misbehave in front of an outsider. Secondly, an outsider can raise his voice or physically restrain the parent if necessary, while a child would never be able to do such things and is not allowed to do so.

Ra'avad's followers reply that it is clear from the end of the story (see the first translation above) that Rav Assi *regretted* having left his mother and therefore the story proves that custodial care is prohibited.[7] Furthermore, if, as Maimonides claims, "others" can take care of the parent, then why can't the child do so himself since he has a better understanding of his parent's desires and idiosyncrasies? In addition, this camp seeks support from R. Jacob ben Asher (1270-1343) who in his code (*Tur, Yoreh Deah* 240) quotes Ra'avad *after* Maimonides, which seems to indicate his agreement with the former. Lastly, this camp asserts that Rav Assi's mother was *not* mentally disturbed but rather old and crotchety. Rav Assi left her because he knew he could not honor her requests properly. But a demented or senile parent needs *extra* physical care from the child while his demented requests can be ignored because he no longer has all of his faculties.

What then are the halakhic options open to a child faced with the dilemma of caring for a parent with Alzheimer's disease? It appears from the above analysis that there are three legitimate halakhic options:

1. A child with stamina and emotional fortitude can follow the line of thought expressed by Ben Sira and advocated by the Ra'avad and his camp. They view "honor thy father and thy mother" as an absolute value which cannot be absolved by the erratic behavior of the parent. Regardless of how the son feels, he must *personally* take care of his parents as commanded by the Torah and must not "leave [them] all the days of his life".

2. Others may place their parent in a nursing home, following the example of Rav Assi as interpreted by Maimonides and his followers. According to this view, a child is not *personally* obligated to care for the parent, if he must sacrifice his own emotional health

in the process. They further state that in cases of mental deterioration, the honor of the parent can be better served by an outsider who can do things the child cannot do and that the parent would not want him to do.

3. Yet I believe the preferred halakhic solution is one implied by a number of the rabbis in the Maimonidean camp – to keep the parent *at home*[8] but pay an outsider to attend to the functions which are painful or inappropriate for the child to perform. This solution incorporates the concerns of both Ra'avad and Maimonides. On the one hand, the parent *feels* wanted and loved by his or her child, a feeling frequently lacking in an institutional setting. The parent functions better at home than in a new and strange environment.[9] By keeping the parent at home, the child fulfills the commandment to "honor your father and your mother" in a direct and personal fashion as demanded by Ra'avad. On the other hand, following Maimonides, the child protects the parent's honor and the child's own emotional health by ensuring that a professional is on hand who can perform functions not in keeping with the honor owed a parent by a child.[10]

NOTES

1. Some four million Americans are now afflicted with Alzheimer's disease – see *Newsweek*, December 18, 1989, pp. 54-63 and March 20, 2000, pp. 48-56; Muriel Gillick, *Tangled Minds: Understanding Alzheimer's Disease*, New York, 1998.
2. *Seder Eliyahu Rabbah*, Chapter (27) 25, ed. Friedmann, p. 136.
3. Two of the three Talmudic passages cited here are aggadic or non-legal in nature. This is not unusual; halakhic authorities frequently rely on non-legal passages in the Talmud when there is a dearth of halakhic sources.
4. *Kiddushin* 31a and cf. *Yerushalmi* ibid., Chapter 1, fol. 61b. According to a parallel passage in *Devarim Rabbah* 14:1, she was *hasrat da'at* – mentally deficient in some way.
5. *Encyclopaedia Judaica*, Vol. 2, col. 346.
6. R. Shem Tov ibn Gaon (fourteenth century), in *Migdal Oz* ad. loc.; R. Nissim Gerondi (1300-1380), on Rif to *Kiddushin*, ed. Vilna, fol. 13a; R. David ibn Zimra (1479-1573) in Radbaz ad. loc.; R. Joseph Karo (1488-1575) in *Shulkhan Arukh Yoreh Deah* 240:10; R. Solomon of Chelm (eighteenth century) in

Mirkevet Hamishneh to Maimonides ad. loc.; R. Yehiel Michal Epstein (1829-1908) in *Arukh Hashulhan, Yoreh Deah* 240:32; and R. Eliezer Waldenberg, *Tzitz Eliezer*, Vol. 12, no. 59.

7. R. Shlomo Luria (1510-1574), *Yam Shel Shlomo* to *Kiddushin*, chapter 1, par. 64; R. Joshua Falk (1555-1614) in *Derishah* to *Tur Yoreh Deah* 240; R. Joel Sirkes (1561-1640) in *Bah* ibid; R. David Halevi (1586-1667) to *Shulkhan Arukh Yoreh Deah* 240:10, subparagraph 14; and R. Samuel Strashun (1794-1872) in *Rashash* to *Kiddushin* ad. loc.
8. The growing phenomenon of adult day care centers enables many children to keep parents with Alzheimer's at home – see *Newsweek*, July 2, 1990, pp. 56-58.
9. *Midrash Hagadol* to *Genesis* 35:6, p. 597 relates that in the ancient city of Luz "when a man became disgusted with his father and mother he would remove them to another city *and immediately they would die*".
10. For further reading, see Gerald Blidstein, *Honor Thy Father and Thy Mother*, New York, 1975, pp. 116-119; Levi Meier, "Filial Responsibility to the 'Senile' Parent" in Levi Meier, ed., *Jewish Values in Bioethics*, New York, 1986, pp. 75-84; Barry Freundel, "*Halakhah* and the Nursing Home Dilemma", *Proceedings of the Association of Orthodox Jewish Scientists* 10 (1990), pp. 85-106.

TORAH STUDY VS. EARNING A LIVING

⁂ YD 246:21 in *Rema* ⁂

Question: *from Edmond H. Weiss, a writer, lecturer and consultant from Cherry Hill, New Jersey: I am perplexed. Lately, my growing interest in Jewish studies has taken so much of my time that I find myself neglecting my business and my clients. Sometimes I resent the time I am forced to spend on "meaningless" work when I could be engaged in study and other mitzvot.*

According to Pirkei Avot (2:2):

> *Rabbai Gamliel says: The study of Torah combined with a worldly occupation is an excellent thing, for the energy needed by both keeps sinful thoughts out of one's mind. And any study of Torah when not accompanied by a trade must fail in the end and become the cause of sin (Avot 2:2).*

Elsewhere, though, this tractate urges "moderation" in business and cautions against using the excuse of business to avoid Torah study.

This is an easier problem, I suspect, for those with salaried jobs because, to a large extent, demands of a job are determined by one's employer. But the self-employed professional or business person is perpetually involved in moral choices: how to organize the day, how much to do, how hard to work and how high to aspire. Moreover, intellectual work demands study, imagination and reflection; creative work can be so depleting that one has no energy for religious study and perhaps not even time to observe the Sabbath. What should one do when the lure of Torah seems like a temptation, a seduction away from one's family responsibilities to earn money and provide for the future?

Responsum: *Limud Torah* [Torah study] is without a doubt one of the central *mitzvot* of Jewish life. We read in the *Shema,* the Torah portion recited three times daily:

> These words which I command you this day shall be in your heart. You shall teach them diligently to your children, speaking of them when you stay at home, when you walk on the road, when you lie down and when you get up (Deuteronomy 6:6-7).

This is repeated in the Prophets: "Let not this book of the Torah cease from your lips, but study it day and night so that you may observe faithfully all that is written in it" (Joshua 1:8). And we learn once again in the Writings: "Happy is the man...the teaching of the Lord is his delight and he studies that teaching day and night" (Psalms 1:1-2).

The centrality of Torah study was reiterated by the rabbis on numerous occasions.[1] "Simon the Just used to say, 'By three things is the world sustained: by the Torah, by the Temple service and by deeds of lovingkindness' " (*Avot* 1:2). "[Hillel] used to say: 'The more Torah, the more life' " (*Avot* 2:7). "Greater is learning the Torah than priesthood or kingship" (*Avot* 6:6). And a popular list of praiseworthy *mitzvot* concludes: "the study of the Torah is equal to them all".[2]

Many Jews are familiar with these quotations. It is, however, less well-known that the Bible and the rabbis had a highly positive view of *melakhah* [labor] and some even viewed it as a *mitzvah*. The prophet Isaiah declares that God teaches the farmers how to farm (Isaiah 28:23-29). The psalmist says: "Happy are all who fear the Lord... you shall enjoy the fruit of your labors" (Psalms 128:1-2). Finally, the Bible condemns idleness on many occasions: "through slothfulness the ceiling sags, through lazy hands the house caves in" (Eccliesiastes 10:18).[3]

The rabbis, too, were staunch advocates of *melakhah*.[4] "Rabbi Judah and Rabbi Shimon said: Great is labor for it honors those who engage in it" *(Nedarim* 49b).

> A person should not say: "I will eat and drink and enjoy the good life and not exert myself and Heaven shall take pity on me". Therefore it is written: "You have blessed the work of his hands" (Job 1:10). A person must toil and work with his hands and then God sends His blessing.[5]

As a result, a trade was considered obligatory by many rabbis: "Rabbi Yishmael said: 'And you shall choose life' (Deuteronomy 30:19) – that is a trade".[6] "We learned in a *beraita* [an early rabbinic source not included in the *Mishnah*]: A father is required to do the following for his son: to circumcise him... to teach him Torah... and to teach him a trade."[7] The rabbis also felt that it is better to engage in a lowly profession than to accept handouts: "Rav said: 'It is better to skin animals in the marketplace and earn wages than to say: "I am a priest, I am a great man, that is beneath my dignity!"'" *(Pesahim* 113a).

Furthermore, in some *midrashim*, labor was given various theological underpinnings:

1. In *Avot d'rabiNatan* we find:

> A person must love labor and engage in labor....If God created the world by doing labor, as it is written, "the work that He had done" (Genesis 2:2), human beings, how much the more so![8]

2. Labor is one of the items included in the covenant with God:

> A person should love *melakhah*...because just as the Torah was given in a covenant, so *melakhah* was given in a covenant, as it is written: "Six days shall you labor and do all your work, but the seventh day is a *Shabbat* for the Lord your God" (Exodus 20:9-10).[9]

3. Since rest on *Shabbat* assumes labor during the week, *melakhah* was even viewed by some rabbis as a positive commandment:

> "Six days shall you labor" (Exodus 20:9) is a separate decree. Just as the Jewish people were commanded to fulfill the positive *mitzvah* of *Shabbat*, so were they commanded regarding labor.[10]

4. The divine presence cannot rest until after labor is complete:

> Great is labor for the *Shekhinah* (God's presence) did not rest upon the Jewish people until they performed *melakhah*, as it is

> written: "And they shall build me a Temple and [only then] shall I dwell in their midst" (Exodus 25:8).[11]

So we see that even though *limud Torah* was considered one of the most basic *mitzvot, melakhah* was also promoted by the rabbis as a basic Jewish value to be respected and practiced.

What then does one do when there is a conflict between Torah study and labor? Which takes precedence? This very issue is discussed in many places in rabbinic literature and, as is frequently the case, there are a variety of contradictory views on the subject. Rabbi Meir says that a person should teach his son an easy and clean trade while Rabbi Nehorai says that he would neglect every trade and teach his son only Torah because one enjoys its reward both in this world and in the World to Come *(Mishnah Kiddushin* 4:14*)*. One man was so anxious for his son to study Torah that he took a vow prohibiting his son from engaging in any form of labor,[12] while Rabban Gamliel said: "Excellent is the study of Torah together with a worldly occupation...but all Torah study without worldly labor comes to naught and leads to sin" *(Avot* 2:2)

But the *locus classicus* is undoubtedly the following:

> Since it says: "And let not this book of the Torah cease from your lips" (Joshua 1:8), I might think that this injunction is to be taken literally. Therefore it says "And you shall gather your grain" (Deuteronomy 11:14) which implies that you are to combine the study of Torah with a worldly occupation – these are the words of Rabbi Yishmael. But Rabbi Shimon bar Yochai says: "if a man plows at plowing time and sows at sowing time and reaps at reaping time...what will become of Torah study? Rather, when Israel does the will of God, their *melakhah* is done by others" *(Berakhot* 35b).

Thus Rabbi Yishmael rules that you should engage in a trade *and* study Torah, while Rabbi Shimon, on the other hand, rules that you should devote all your time to *limud Torah* and God will provide. What is the *halakhah*? The *gemara* concludes: "Abaye said: 'Many followed Rabbi Yishmael and succeeded, many followed Rabbi Shimon bar Yochai and did not succeed'". Abaye's opinion was followed by the major codes of Jewish law.[13] Furthermore, we know that dozens of Talmudic rabbis such as Shimon ben Shetach, Abba Shaul, Rabbi Joshua, Rabbi Judah, Rabbi Yose, Resh Lakish, Rabbi Zeira, Rav Huna, Rav Hisda and Abaye supported themselves through manual labor.[14] So we see that despite all of the opinions on the subject, the halakhic ideal is that of Rabbi Yishmael: Engage in a trade *and* study Torah.

What remains is the practical question: How do I organize my time so that I can earn a living *and* study Torah? The following four suggestions are culled from 2,000 years of Jewish experience:

1. Rabbi Yose ben Meshullam and Rabbi Shimon ben Menasya were part of a group called "the Holy Congregation" "who divided their day in three – they devoted one-third to Torah, one-third to prayer and one-third to *melakhah*".[15] According to this source, one should devote an *equal* portion of every day to earning a living and to Torah study. This, of course, depends on a person's profession. In many professions, one cannot devote such a large chunk of time to Torah study without harming one's livelihood. Indeed, that is probably why the practice is attributed to "the Holy Congregation"!

2. This objective difficulty no doubt led to Rabbi Joshua's more lenient opinion:

> If a person learns two *halakhot* by heart every morning and two every evening and engages in *melakhah* all day, he is considered to have fulfilled the entire Torah.[16]

In other words, quantity is not everything. If you don't have time to study many hours a day, just make sure to study on a regular basis. This approach was widely followed throughout Jewish history and led to the creation of countless fellowships *(havarot)* that met daily to study Torah. In Eastern Europe Jews preferred *Mishnah*, Talmud, *Hayye Adam* or *Mishnah Berurah;* in Yemen they studied *Mishnah*, Talmud, Maimonides and *Ein Ya'akov*.[17] In our own day, thousands of Jews study a daily chapter of Bible or *Mishnah* or a daily folio of Talmud *(daf yomi)*.[18] You can adopt this system of Torah study by joining an already existing study group, starting a new one or finding a study partner *(havruta)* for daily Torah study.

3. A third approach is to earn a living by day and study by night. This was the approach favored by Maimonides as described in a famous responsum detailing his exhausting schedule as court physician, from which it is clear that he did all of his studying at night.[19] This was in keeping with the opinion of many Talmudic rabbis who preferred nighttime study to daytime study.[20]

4. Lastly, there was the system of *Yarhei Kallah* practiced in Babylon for close to a millennium, in which thousands of laypeople and students gathered in the Babylonian academies during the Hebrew months of Elul and Adar to study Torah *(Bava Metzia 86a; Berakhot* 17b). This system continued to flourish until the days of Rabbi Nattan Habavli (tenth century). A modern equivalent would be to spend the summer studying Torah at a camp or a retreat, at a *yeshivah* in Israel or at a Jewish studies program such as the one run by the Jewish Theological Seminary in New York.

In conclusion, learning Torah is a *mitzvah* and earning a livelihood is a *mitzvah,* but you should not go overboard in observing one at the expense of the other. Choose, rather, the middle road. As we learn in the Palestinian Talmud:

> This Torah is like two paths, one of fire and one of snow. If you follow one path, you will die of heat; if you follow the other path you will die of cold. What should you do? Take the middle path![21]

NOTES

1. For 881 Talmudic statements (sic!) in praise of Torah and Torah study, see Rabbi Moshe David Gross, *Otzar Ha-aggadah,* vol. 3, Jerusalem, 1977, pp. 1357-1382.
2. *Pe'ah* 1:1 and Philip Birnbaum, ed., *Daily Prayer Book,* New York, 1949, p. 15.
3. For fifteen similar passages in the book of Proverbs, see *The Universal Jewish Encyclopedia,* vol. 6, p. 499.
4. For a recent and thorough treatment of this topic, see Meir Ayali, *Workers and Artisans: Their Occupations and Status in Rabbinic Literature* (Hebrew),

Givatayim, 1987, chapter 4 and see p. 193, ibid., for twelve previous books on the subject.

5. *Tanhuma Vayeitzei,* par. 13.
6. *Yerushalmi Sotah* 9:16, fol. 24c.
7. *Kiddushin* 29a and parallels.
8. *Avot d'rabi Natan,* Version B, chapter 21, ed. Schechter, p. 44.
9. Ibid., Version A, Chapter 11, p. 44.
10. *Mekhilta of Rabbi Shimon Bar Yochai,* ed. Epstein-Melamed, p. 149.
11. Ibid.
12. *Tosefta Bekhorot* 6:11, ed. Zuckermandel, p. 541.
13. Maimonides, *Talmud Torah* 3:10-11; *Tur* and *Shulhan Arukh Yoreh De'ah* 246:21 and *Orah Hayyim* 156:1.
14. For a survey of occupations practiced by Talmudic rabbis, see Ayali, *Workers and Artisans,* pp. 100-101 and 143-151, and Moses Aberbach, *Labor, Crafts and Commerce in Ancient Israel,* Jerusalem, 1994, Chapter III.
15. *Kohelet Rabbah* 9:9, ed. Vilna, fol. 24a. Regarding "the Holy Congregation", see Shmuel Safrai, *Eretz Yisrael V'hakhameha Bitkufat Hamishnah Vehatalmud,* Jerusalem, 1983, pp. 43-56.
16. *Mekhilta of Rabbi Yishmael, Vayassa,* ed. Lauterbach, vol. 2, pp. 103-104.
17. For Eastern Europe, see Mark Zborowski and Elizabeth Herzog, *Life is with People: The Jewish Little Towns of Eastern Europe,* New York, 1952, pp. 100-102; A.J. Heschel, *The Earth is the Lord's,* Philadelphia, 1963, pp. 46-47; and Israel Goldman, *Lifelong Learning Among the Jews,* New York, 1975, Chapter 10. For Yemen, see Shimon Garidi, *Torah Study in Yemen* (Hebrew), Jerusalem, 1987.
18. *Daf yomi,* instituted by Rabbi Meir Shapira in 1923, has resulted in completing the entire Talmud (ca. 2,700 folios!) ten times.
19. For an English translation, see Franz Kobler, *Letters of Jews through the Ages,* vol. 1, Philadelphia, 1978, pp. 211-212.
20. *Song of Songs Rabbah 5:*1, ed Vilna, fol. 31a; *Hagigah* 12b; *Avodah Zarah 3b; Sanhedrin* 92a; Maimonides, *Talmud Torah* 3:13 and *Shulhan Arukh Yoreh De'ah 246:23*
21. *Yerushalmi Hagigah* 2:1, 77a and *Tosefta Hagigah* 2:5, ed. Lieberman, p. 381. That passage refers specifically to the study of Jewish mysticism, but the same holds true of many things in life. For recent discussions of the topic of this responsum, see Aberbach (above, note 14), Chapter IV, and Leo Levi, *Tradition* 28/1 (Fall 1993), pp. 46-81.

INVESTIGATING THE CHARITIES TO WHICH WE CONTRIBUTE

YD 251:10; 256:1; 257:2

Question: *A bag lady accosts me on the Upper West Side of Manhattan and asks me for a quarter. Should I ask her why she doesn't go out and get a job? A schnorer [charity collector] knocks on my door, holds out a letter signed by an eminent rabbi and asks me to contribute to his yeshivah in Jerusalem. Should I check out the letter and the yeshivah? I enter my local Jewish bookstore and see five pushkes [charity boxes] on the counter. Should I automatically put a quarter in each, or should I read the fine print and investigate each charity's legitimacy? Lastly, I receive many direct mail solicitations every month. Should I send a small donation to each, or investigate every charity that asks for money and send a larger contribution to the one that deserves it most?*

Responsum: Jews have been grappling with these dilemmas for at least 2,000 years. On the one hand, most individuals and organizations that ask for our help are legitimate and really do merit our *tzedakah*. On the other hand, a certain percentage of those who ask for money are charlatans and crooks.

Some *tzedakah* experts say that giving is a habit that must be cultivated. Therefore, it is better to give often and spontaneously, even if one is not sure about the credentials of the recipients because, if we stop to think about every contribution, we will get out of the *tzedahah* habit. Others say we should investigate before we give, because by giving to the wrong people and organizations, we may have technically fulfilled the *mitzvah* of *tzedakah*, but we are in fact depriving those who really need our help.[1] Let us see what Jewish tradition has to say on the subject.

Surprisingly enough, the rabbinic sources have a basically positive attitude toward beggars.[2] Maimonides clearly states:

> Whoever sees a poor person asking [for assistance] and ignores him and does not give him *tzedakah* has transgressed a negative commandment as it is written "do not harden you heart nor shut your hand against your needy brother" (Deuteronomy 15:7).[3]

We do not know the talmudic source of this statement, but it is clearly in keeping with the following rabbinic passage:

> Rabbi Abin said: This poor person stands at your door and the Holy One blessed be He stands at his right hand as it is written: "He stands at the right hand of the needy" (Psalms 109:31). (*Vayikra Rabbah* 34:9)

On the other hand, other passages recommend kindness to beggars for selfish reasons: "Rabbi Nahman said: This world is like a water wheel – the bucket that is full empties while the empty becomes filled' " (ibid. and parallels). In other words, you should give to beggars now, because one day down the road the tables may be turned – the beggar may become wealthy while you may become a beggar.

Nonetheless, our sages were not blind. They knew that some beggars were frauds and, even if investigated, some would escape detection. Indeed, a number of rabbis were duped by dishonest beggars. Rabbi Hanina, for example,

> was accustomed to send four *zuz* to a certain poor person every *Erev Shabbat* [Friday]. One time he sent the money with his wife. She returned and said to him, "There is no need... I heard them say to him: 'On what will you dine – on the white linen tablecloths or on the dyed silk tablecloths?' "[4]

This type of fraud prompted Rabbi Elazar to say: "Come let us be grateful to the cheaters, for were it not for them we [who do not always respond to every appeal for *tzedakah*] would sin every day".[5]

Other sages were not so forgiving. They resorted to cursing the cheaters in order to discourage fraud. The *Mishnah (Pe'ah* 8:9), for example, states:

> Whoever does not need to take yet takes, will not depart from

> the world until he will be dependent on others... and whoever is not lame or blind and pretends to be, will not die of old age before he becomes like one of them, as it is written: "He who seeks evil, upon him it shall come" (Proverbs 11:27).[6]

This warning was reiterated in four other places in rabbinic literature[7] and was codified in the standard codes of Jewish law.[8]

Yet, despite the fear of possible fraud, *none* of the sages refrained from giving *tzedakah.* After all, it is a positive commandment (Deuteronomy 15:7-11) that, according to Rav Assi, is as important as all of the other commandments put together *(Bava Batra* 9a). Some later rabbis shared the liberal approach of Rabbi Chaim of Tzanz, a nineteenth-century hassidic rabbi:

> I give *tzedakah* to one hundred poor people on the assumption that I may find one out of a hundred who is worthy and I will have the merit of helping him. But you refrain from giving to one hundred poor people... lest one of them be unworthy. Therefore know that the average beggar who holds out his hand is presumed to need the money and you should not concern yourself with hidden matters.[9]

The talmudic sages, however, were more careful with their *tzedahah.* They realized that if you give to everyone who *asks* for money, you ultimately deprive those who really *need* the money. They therefore took precautions against fraudulent beggars:

1. Rabbi Sheilah of Naveh made a play on the word "*ha'evyon*" [a needy person]: "This needy person *hav hunakh* [beware] of him." In other words, beware of cheaters. (*Vayikra Rabbah* 34:9)

2. Rabbi Abbah did not want to embarrass the poor by having to look at them, following the principle of *mattan baseter* [giving in secret] (*Bava Batra* 9b and 10b), but he was wary of cheaters. He therefore would wrap the coins in his kerchief and drag it behind him and walk by the houses of the poor, but out of the corner of his eye he looked for cheaters *(Ketubot* 67b).

3. There is one talmudic passage that gives explicit advice about avoiding charity fraud:[10] "Rav Huna said: 'One investigates when

asked for food, but not when asked for clothing'". The Talmud explains that in his opinion, clothing is more urgent than food because it causes the beggar shame and should therefore be supplied, no questions asked. "Rav Yehudah, however, said: One investigates when asked for clothing, but not when asked for food.'" The Talmud explains that in his opinion, lack of food is more urgent than lack of clothing because it causes physical pain and suffering and should therefore be supplied without investigation. The Talmud concludes with a *beraita* [teaching of the early sages] which supports Rav Yehudah and this latter ruling was codified by the standard codes of Jewish law.[11]

It seems, then, that the guiding principle was that one waives investigation when faced with an urgent situation of human suffering: A person who asks for food may be in pain and may die. Therefore, you give him the benefit of the doubt and feed him on the spot. But a person who asks for a change of clothes can wait while you check him out.

Times have changed and beggars no longer ask for food or clothing, but the same principle can be applied: If an emaciated person dressed in rags asks you for a quarter, you should give him the benefit of the doubt. But if a nicely dressed *schnorer* comes to your door collecting for his *yeshivah,* you can take down his particulars and send him a check *after* checking out his legitimacy. No one will starve in the interim.

All of the sources quoted thus far have dealt with *individuals* who ask for money. What of *organizations* that today do most of their solicitation through *pushkes* or via the mail? How can we determine their legitimacy? The *halakhah* provides two clear criteria: The trustworthiness of the *gabbai* or collector – today that means the person who runs the charity – and the financial records of the organization.[12]

The Talmud states:

> A person should not give a penny to the communal charity purse unless it is under the supervision of a person [as honest as] Rabbi Hananyah ben Teradyon *(Bava Batra* 10b and *Avodah Zarah* 17b).

Rabbi Hananyah was chosen as the paradigm because once, when the funds of two different charities became confused, he made up the difference from his own pocket *(Avodah Zarah* ibid.). The standard codes of Jewish law therefore rule that "a person should only give to a charity fund if he knows that the overseer is trustworthy and wise and knows how to manage it properly".[13] In most cases, if the person running the organization is trustworthy, then the organization is trustworthy. People trust Yad Sarah in Jerusalem because they trust Uri Lupoliansky. People trust Hadassah because they trust the women who run it. People trust the Muscular Dystrophy Foundation because they trust Jerry Lewis.

As for financial records, the Talmud states: "One does not check the records of *tzedakah* collectors... as it is written [regarding the treasurers of the Temple]: 'for they do their work in good faith' " (II Kings 12:16) *(Bava Batra* 9a). Maimonides (9:11) and Rabbi Joseph Karo (*YD* 257:2) simply quote the Talmud. But Rabbi Jacob ben Asher and Rabbi Moshe Isserles have a different approach *(Tur* and *Shulhan Arukh YD,* ibid.):

> One does not need to investigate honest collectors. But in order that they be "clean before the Lord and before Israel" (Numbers 32:22), it is good for them to give an accounting.

They knew what many *tzedakah* experts stress: Accountability leads to honesty and efficiency. It is hard to cheat when everyone has access to the facts and figures. It is hard to waste money on overhead, when potential donors know exactly how much is being spent on furniture, staff and brochures.

Thus, according to the *halakhah,* when you see a *pushke* or receive a mail solicitation, your first question should be: Do I trust the person running the organization? If you do not know the *gabbai* or cannot find out enough about him, you should request a copy of the budget in order to check the group's honesty and wastefulness.

In conclusion, giving *tzedakah* is good, but giving wisely is even better. As *tzedakah* expert Danny Siegel writes:

> You are not doing this out of a sense of cynicism. You are protecting your *tzedakah* dollars, making them stretch as far as

they can go to worthy causes...On the one hand, you do not want to give to wasteful organizations... On the other hand, you would not want to withhold useful, perhaps critical, *tzedakah* money from people who are laboring with love and care to make good things happen in this world.[14]

NOTES

1. For both approaches, see Haim Shapiro, "Duties of the Heart," *The Jerusalem Post Magazine,* May 3, 1991, pp. 14-17.
2. See *Encyclopaedia Judaica, s.v.* "Begging and Beggars", and Arthur Kurzweil "The Treatment of Beggars in Jewish Tradition," in *Gym Shoes and Irises* by Danny Siegel, Spring Valley, New York, 1982, pp. 103-117. It should be added that the Bible too extols the virtues of feeding and clothing the poor (e.g. Isaiah 58:7, 10 and Ezekiel 18:7, 16), but it makes no explicit reference to the treatment of beggars.
3. Gifts to the Poor 7:2. All further references to Maimonides in this responsum refer to this section of his code. For a similar approach, see *Vayikra Rabbah* 34:9, ed. Margaliot, pp. 791-793.
4. *Ketubot* 67b-68a; cf. *Vayikra Rabbah* 34:10, pp. 793-794 and *Yerushalmi Pe'ah* 8:9, ed. Venice 21b.
5. ibid.
6. The verse from Proverbs is only found in some versions of the *Mishnah.*
7. *Tosefta Pe'ah* 4:14, ed. Lieberman, p. 59; *Yerushalmi Pe'ah* 8:9, 21b; *Bavli Ketubot 68a;* and *Avot D'rabbi Nattan,* Version A, Chapter 3, ed. Schechter, 8a.
8. Maimonides 10:19; *Tur Yoreh De'ah* [hereafter: *YD*] *255; Shulhan Arukh YD* 255:2.
9. *Darkei Hayyim,* Jerusalem, 1962, p. 137.
10. *Bava Batra* 9a; cf. *Yerushalmi Pe'ah 8:7,* 21a and *Vayikra Rabbah* 34:14, p. 802.
11. Maimonides 7:6; *Tur YD* 251; *Shulhan Arukh YD* 251:10.
12. These are the same criteria stressed by Danny Siegel in "Which *Tzedakah* Should You Send Checks To? Ten Steps to Making an Intelligent Decision," *Baltimore Jewish Times,* Feb. 8, 1991, pp. 3, 10.
13. Maimonides 10:8 and cf. 9:1; *Tur YD* 256; *Shulhan Arukh YD* 256:1; Rashi to *Pesahim* 49b, catchword *gabba'ei tzedakah.*
14. Siegel, "Which *Tzedakah*". For a similar approach, see Dr. Eliezer Jaffe, *Giving Wisely,* Jerusalem, 1982, p. 27. For other discussions of this topic, see Barry Holtz, *Finding Our Way: Jewish Texts and the Lives We Live Today,* New York, 1990, pp. 170-176; David Assaf in: Moshe Ishon, ed. *Itturim... in Honor of Moshe Krone,* Jerusalem, 5746, pp. 248-262; R. Naftali Zvi Yehudah Bar-Ilan, *Sefer Nikdash Bitzdakah,* Rehovot, 5751, pp. 201-210; R. Yonah Metzger, *Miyam Hahalakhah,* Vol. 4, Tel Aviv, 5753, No. 79.

TELLING THE TRUTH TO TERMINAL PATIENTS

YD 337:1

Question: *Many of us have relatives and friends who have been diagnosed with inoperable cancer or another fatal disease. Does Jewish law require us to tell them the truth about their condition? Is telling the truth a mitzvah that must be fulfilled at all costs? Do patients have a "right to know"? What principles should guide us in deciding how much to reveal to them?*

Responsum: Telling the truth is not necessarily one of the 613 commandments,[1] but it is without a doubt a very basic Jewish value. The Bible instructs us repeatedly: "Keep far from a false matter" (Exodus 23:7); "You shall not steal, neither shall you deal falsely, nor lie to one another" (Leviticus 19:11); "Speak the truth to one another" (Zekhariah 8:16); "Remove all false ways from me" (Psalms 119:29). The *Mishnah* adds: "The world rests on three pillars: on justice, on truth and on peace" (*Avot* 1:18).

Does this mean that *halakhah* prohibits all forms of lying? Not at all. Unlike Augustine, Aquinas and Kant, who view truth as an absolute value,[2] Jewish tradition permits lying when the motive is altruistic – for the sake of peace, modesty, protecting other people's feelings and their physical safety. For example, it is permissible to lie for the sake of peace (*Yevamot* 65b and *Bava Metzia* 87a): When Sarah heard she would have a son, "she laughed to herself, saying, 'Now that I am withered, am I to have enjoyment – *with my husband so old?'* " God changed Sarah's insulting remarks when repeating them to Abraham: "Shall I in truth bear a child, *old as I am?"* (Genesis 18:12-13). Similarly, it is permissible to stretch the truth when praising an ugly bride at her wedding (*Ketubot* 16b-17a) and to make a false vow to a robber or murderer (*Mishnah Nedarim* 3:4). Lastly,

> in three things rabbis may deviate from the truth: regarding their knowledge [so as not to boast], regarding their sexual relations with their wives [out of modesty] and about their host [so he will not be inundated with freeloaders] (*Bava Metzia* 23b-24a).

Thus, in theory, we may certainly conceal the truth from terminally ill patients *if it is for their own good,* since Judaism commands us to do everything to heal and preserve the life of the patient.[3] The dilemma, therefore, is not "may we lie to terminally ill patients", but rather "is lying to terminally ill patients good or bad for them". On the one hand, if we lie about their condition, patients may retain their good spirits, but they will not be able to take leave of their families in the proper fashion or put their affairs in order. On the other hand, if we tell the truth, patients will be able to say goodbye and attend to their affairs, but their lives may be shortened by the shock and depression brought on by the naked truth.

As is frequently the case, a number of our classic sources have already dealt with this ethical dilemma. A few sources clearly prefer lying in order to protect patients:

1. In II Kings 8:7-15, Ben-Hadad, King of Aram, is taken ill. He sends his minister, Hazael, to the prophet Elisha to inquire of the Lord: "Will I recover from this illness?" Hazael went to meet [Elisha]... "Your son, King Ben-Hadad of Aram, has sent me to you to ask: Will I recover from this illness?' " Elisha said to him: "*Go and say to him: 'You will recover'. However, the Lord has revealed to me that he will die".*

Hazael then repeats the lie to Ben-Hadad, who dies on the morrow.

2. In Isaiah 38 and II Kings 20, the prophet Isaiah bluntly informs King Hezekiah of his imminent death:

> In those days Hezekiah became deathly ill. The prophet Isaiah son of Amotz came to him and said: "Thus said the Lord: 'Set your affairs in order *for you are going to die, you will not live'* ".

Hezekiah thereupon prays to God, who forgives him and adds fifteen years to his life. The *midrash* strongly condemns Isaiah for his behavior:

> Said Hezekiah to Isaiah: "Normally, when a person visits the sick, he says: 'May the Heavens have compassion upon you'...and even if it is obvious that he is about to die, one does not tell a sick person to put his house in order *that he might not experience mental distress.* And yet you tell me: 'Set your affairs in order for you are going to die, you will not live'! I will not...listen to your words! Instead I will rely on my ancestor Solomon who said: 'Fear God'" (Ecclesiastes 5:6) [and then Hezekiah repented].[4]

3. Finally, from a similar situation it seems that the Talmud would also favor deception:

> Our rabbis taught: A sick person whose close relative has died – one does not inform him of the death lest he be emotionally overwhelmed.[5]

If one withholds information from patients about the death of a loved one because of emotional distress, one should certainly withhold information from patients about their own terminal illness.

On the other hand, two medieval sources clearly favor full disclosure.

1. We read in *Sefer Hassidim* [The Book of the Pious], written in thirteenth century Germany, regarding

> an expert physician who knows how to determine from a patient's urine or by other methods if a patient will die. If the patient says: "Don't conceal anything from me! You are only [lying] in order not to upset me, but I would be much happier to know the truth!" If he does not want to live because he is in great pain or if he is very old – the physician should tell him the truth. Or if the patient needs to take care of his affairs, the physician should tell him: "Have no fear, but in any case take care of your affairs." And if he sees that the patient does not wish to know,[6] he should [nonetheless] tell him, as it is

> written: "Set your affairs in order; for you are going to die, you will not live" (II Kings 20:1).[7]

2. A similar opinion was expressed by Amatus Lusitanus, a famous Jewish physician, in his medical oath, penned in 1559:

> If I speak falsehood, may God and his angel Raphael punish me with their eternal wrath and may no one henceforth place trust in me.[8]

Today, this issue has been extensively debated by *halakhic* authorities. Those who favor withholding information or deceiving the patient, rely on Elisha and *Midrash Rabbah* as their precedents,[9] while those who favor telling the truth rely on *Sefer Hassidim*.[10]

It is worth noting that both points of view are found in non-Jewish sources as well. Physicians such as Hippocrates in the fifth century b.c.e., Galen in the second century c.e. and Drs. Thomas Percival and Oliver Wendell Holmes in the nineteenth recommended concealing the truth from a terminally ill patient.[11] Indeed, this was the approach of most doctors until the 1960s. The medieval church, on the other hand, insisted on telling the patient the naked truth in order to enable him to confess and prepare for death.[12]

Since the 1970s, however, physicians have had a drastic change of heart. Thus, for example, in 1961, 88% of the doctors at one hospital in Chicago were *opposed* to disclosing the truth to a cancer patient,[13] while in 1979, 98% of the doctors at a hospital in Rochester were in *favor* of such disclosure![14] We do not know about patient attitudes in the past, but since 1950, 80-98% of patients surveyed in the U.S. said they wanted to know the truth.[15] This drastic change is the result of many factors. Doctors are more willing to discuss cancer since therapies have improved and there is greater hope for recovery. They frequently need the patient's consent and cooperation in order to administer the appropriate therapy. They are less afraid of discussing death because they better understand the process of dying. On the other hand, patients frequently guess the diagnosis since there is greater public awareness about fatal diseases and it is better for them to hear the prognosis from their physician than to imagine the worst. Finally, patients today insist on their right to know and to be part of the decision-making process.

Therefore it is clear that we cannot divorce the Jewish sources from their sociological and psychological context. Elisha may have lied to Ben-Hadad because in his day *that* was considered best for the patient, while the author of *Sefer Hassidim* advocated telling the truth because in his day *that* was considered best for the patient. Thus today it is not sufficient to quote Elisha and studies from the 1950s and 1960s[16] because the sociological reality has changed. Today, we must follow *Sefer Hassidim* and the statistics of *today* as Dr. Avraham Steinberg has suggested:

> In all likelihood, one should determine the halakhic attitude to this problem in consonance with the time and the place. If at one time there is a greater expectation and readiness to know the truth, then its transmittal will assist the patient. And the opposite holds true – in a time and place where there is great fear of the truth, then it should not be told.[17]

Therefore, since most patients today *want* to know the truth, the *halakhah* mandates telling them the truth. This is not necessarily because they have the "right to know", but because, as of today, this information has proved beneficial and therapeutic. Roughly 4-7% of patients, however, do *not* wish to know the truth.[18] Doctors and families must use their best judgment to ensure that such patients are *not* told the truth because the truth would be harmful to them.

Most experts agree that the main issue today is not *whether* to tell patients but *how* to tell patients. They stress that patients should be told by their own physician, *after* all the medical facts are known, in a private place, in plain English and in as gentle and as hopeful a fashion as possible.[19] Needless to say, these are only general guidelines. In the final analysis, "*each case must be judged on its own merits according to the individual patient.*"[20]

NOTES

1. See Mark Dratch, *Judaism* 37/2 (Spring 1988), pp. 225-226 and J. David Bleich in Fred Rosner, ed., *Medicine and Jewish Law*, Northvale, New Jersey, 1990, pp. 52-53.
2. See Dratch, pp. 218-219, and Sissela Bok in *Encylopedia of Bioethics*, New York, 1978, pp. 1684-1686.
3. See, for example, J. David Bleich, *Judaism and Healing: Halakhic Perspectives*, New York, 1981, chapter 1, and Fred Rosner, *Modern Medicine and Jewish Ethics*, Hoboken and New York, 1986, chapter 1.
4. *Kohelet Rabbah* 5:6, ed. Vilna 14d and cf. *Berakhot* 10a.
5. *Moed Kattan* 26b and *Yoreh Deah* 337:1.
6. The Hebrew original is garbled. I have translated according to the context.
7. *Sefer Hassidim*, ed. Berlin, 1891, p. 66, par. 154. For the halakhic importance of this work, see Louis Jacobs, *A Tree of Life*, Oxford, 1984, pp. 72, 79-80. Rabbi Bleich's effort to belittle the importance of this source in *Medicine and Jewish Law*, pp. 60-61 is not convincing.
8. Harry Friedenwald, *The Jews and Medicine*, vol. 1, Baltimore, 1944, p. 368.
9. Bleich, *Judaism and Healing*, chapter 4 and Bleich, *Medicine and Jewish Law*, pp. 31-63; Basil Herring, *Jewish Ethics and Halakhah for Our Time*, vol. 1, New York, 1984, chapter 2 and the literature cited by Avraham Steinberg, *Halakhic-Medical Encyclopedia*, second edition, vol. 1, Jerusalem, 1988, cols. 142-143.
10. Rosner, chapter 6; Gary Lavit, *Journal of Halacha and Contemporary Society* XV (Spring 1988), pp. 94-124; Steinberg and the literature cited by him, cols. 143-144. For a non-Jewish advocate of disclosure, see Sissela Bok, *Lying: Moral Choice in Public and Private Life*, New York, 1978, chapter 15.
11. Rabbi Immanuel Jakobovits, *Jewish Medical Ethics*, New York, 1959, p. 121 and especially S. J. Reiser, *Annals of Internal Medicine* 92 (1980), pp. 837-842.
12. Jakobovits, ibid.
13. D. Oken, *Journal of the American Medical Association* 175 (1961), pp. 1120-1128.
14. Dennis Novack et al., ibid., 241 (1979), pp. 897-900.
15. R. M. Veatch, *Encyclopedia of Bioethics*, p. 1678 and Bok, *Lying*, p. 229 and note 11.
16. See Bleich, *Judaism and Healing* and Bleich, *Medicine and Jewish Law*, who primarily quotes anecdotes and studies from the 1950s and 1960s.
17. Steinberg, p. 144, end of note 78.
18. Bleich, *Medicine and Jewish Law*, p. 44, note 9; Steinberg, col. 138, note 11; and Lavit, p. 106, note 32. It should be stressed that the studies quoted are from 1959 and 1962 and are probably dated. For a recent study in Israel, see *The*

Jerusalem Post, October 4, 1998, p. 11 where 6% of terminal patients surveyed did *not* wish to know the truth.

19. Rosner, pp. 62-64; Lavit; Steinberg, cols. 139-140; Bleich, *Medicine and Jewish Law*, pp. 61-63; Thurstan Brewin, *The Lancet* 337 (May 18, 1991), pp. 1207-1209; and Timothy Quill, *Archives of Internal Medicine* 151 (March 1991), pp. 463-468, which includes an extensive bibliography.
20. Steinberg, col. 144, end of note 78. For an extensive bibliography on this topic, see the Hebrew version of this responsum, *Et La'asot* 4 (Winter 1996), pp. 48-49.

RESPONSA RELATED TO EVEN HA'EZER

GENETIC ENGINEERING

EH 2:7

Question: *Does Jewish law permit genetic engineering on human beings?*

Responsum: Until recently it was assumed that human beings are created by their fathers and mothers and by God. As we read in the *Mishnah* (*Eduyot* 2:9): "A father endows his son with beauty, strength, wealth, wisdom and longevity...". So too, are we taught in the Talmud (*Niddah* 31a):

> Our sages have taught: There are three partners in a man – The Holy One, blessed be He, his father and his mother. His father sows the white substance out of which are formed the child's bones, sinews, nails, the brain in his head and the white of the eye. His mother supplies the red substance out of which is formed the child's skin, flesh, hair and the black of the eye. The Holy One, blessed be He, gives him breath, spirit, facial appearance, sight, hearing, speech, mobility, wisdom and understanding.

And finally the *midrash* states:

> Said Rabbi Elazar in the name of R. Yossi ben Zimra: were all the nations of the world to gather together to create even one mosquito, they could not give it a soul... (*Genesis Rabbah* 39:14)

This basic assumption has been called into question by various types of medical and laboratory procedures that have been developed during this century and especially during the past twenty years. Suddenly, the doctor and the geneticist have become active partners in the creation of human life through artificial insemination, sex preselection, test-tube babies, host mothers, recombinant DNA technology, cloning and different types of genetic engineering. Indeed, all of these topics have been dealt with by rabbis and halakhic authorities.[1] We shall confine ourselves here to genetic engineering, which Dr. William French Anderson of the National Institutes of Health (NIH) has divided into four categories:[2]

1. "Somatic cell gene therapy" aims to correct a genetic defect or other disease in the somatic [body] cells of a patient by removing defective bone marrow from a patient, inserting normal genes in some cells and re-implanting them in the patient. Scientists have used this procedure since 1989 to treat genetic diseases such as the immuno-deficiency syndrome ADA, as well as AIDS and certain types of cancer, and they are hopeful that they will be able to use gene therapy to treat many single-gene diseases such as hemophilia, Gaucher's disease, cystic fibrosis, thalassemia and sickle-cell anemia.[3]

2. "Germ line gene therapy" would require the insertion of the normal gene into the reproductive tissue of the patient in such a way that the genetic disorder would also be corrected in his or her offspring. This type of gene therapy has been successfully achieved with mice, but many obstacles remain before it can be used in human beings.[4]

3. "Enhancement genetic engineering" would insert a gene in a healthy person in order to effect a non-therapeutic change in his height, eye color or hair color. This type of genetic engineering is now technically feasible for somatic cells, but has not been attempted both for medical and ethical reasons.[5]

4. "Eugenic genetic engineering" would attempt to improve or alter complex human traits such as personality or intelligence, each of which is coded by a large number of genes. This remains at present a distant, theoretical possibility.[6]

While all but the first of these techniques do not yet exist, many ethicists and rabbis have warned that we should discuss and debate these issues now, before the fact, rather than deal with a fait accompli. This need was eloquently expressed by Dr. Marc Lappe as far back as 1978:

> Genetics is going to revolutionize our lives. Social institutions and legal traditions that we have taken for granted will be shaken to their roots... I am convinced that any grasp of these radical shifts will require each of us to become a moral investigator as well as a scientific one. That means going beyond the constraints of science into the world of human emotions and beliefs.[7]

Similar words of warning were expressed by Rabbi Walter Jacob, a prominent Reform halakhic authority:

> We are standing at the edge of a new scientific era. We certainly wish to utilize the potentials of genetic engineering for the benefit of humanity... As we learn more about the nature of genetic engineering we must discuss its moral implications both with regard to animals and human beings... So we must proceed with caution. In consort with others, we must set limits and provide direction...[8]

After these cuationary remarks, let us return to the four types of genetic engineering described above:

It seems quite clear that both somatic and germ-line gene therapy are entirely in keeping with Jewish law and tradition; indeed, this has been the conclusion of all the halakhic authorities who have dealt with the issue.[9] The idea of avoiding hereditary diseases and genetic problems finds support in three rabbinic sources:

> Rava said: ... a man should not marry a woman from a family of epileptics or lepers, providing that the disease has occurred three times in that family *(Yevamot* 64b).

> Said Resh Lakish: a tall man should not marry a tall woman lest they give birth to a giant; a male dwarf should not marry a female dwarf lest they give birth to an even smaller dwarf; a very pale man should not marry a very pale woman lest they give birth to an albino; a very swarthy man should not marry

a very swarthy woman lest they give birth to a child who is pitch black *(Bekhorot* 45b).

Despite the fact that the Talmud recommends marrying a niece *(Yevamot* 62b = *Sanhedrin* 76b), the medieval Testament attributed to Rabbi Judah the Pious says that "a man should not marry his niece or his nephew", a ruling that was later codified by many authorities.[10] This ruling was no doubt the result of observing that such marriages led to various genetic diseases.

Thus, since our sages were careful to avoid genetic problems, they would no doubt have approved of gene therapy that aims to eliminate hereditary diseases both before and after birth.

Furthermore, Judaism wholeheartedly supports medicine and medical research because they seek to eliminate every kind of disease.[11] Therefore, Jewish law supports gene therapy that seeks to eliminate serious or fatal genetic diseases.

Finally, it stands to reason that any surgery permitted on a *person* should be permitted on a *gene* before conception. Thus, for example, if a surgical cure for hemophilia were possible, it would surely be permissible; so too, it would be permissible to cure hemophilia by gene surgery.[12]

And what of enhancement or eugenic engineering for non-therapeutic reasons? May we strive to engineer children with blond hair and blue eyes, or children who will grow to be seven feet tall and play basketball, or piano virtuosi, or people with an IQ of 220? Here, too, one could look for some sort of biblical or talmudic precedent to permit these types of genetic engineering.[13] But ultimately one would have to agree with the three rabbis who have expressed opposition to this line of research.[14]

Jewish law as it now stands does not forbid these practices, but I believe they should be forbidden as a *gezeirah,* or rabbinic prohibition,[15] because they are not in keeping with Jewish ethics and theology. First of all, our understanding of how the human body and mind work is still elementary. We simply do not know the effect on the entire body or mind of altering one gene or a series of genes.[16] While we can justify gene therapy to eliminate serious or fatal disease, we cannot justify it for its own sake. Secondly, societies have historically abused their power in the pursuit of eugenic goals.[17] As Jews, we must be doubly sensitive to eugenics, which was practiced by Nazi doctors in their quest for a master race.[18] Furthermore, these types of genetic engineering are a "slippery slope". Once we begin to create smarter, taller and stronger children, there will be no way of setting limits.[19] We could end up with man-made freaks of all sorts. We must forbid these types of genetic engineering following the rabbinic concept of *lo plug (Bava Metzia* 53b), which forbids something across the board without differentiating between various cases.

Lastly, just because human beings are *capable* of doing something does not mean they *should* do something. We are told in the Bible that human beings were created in the image of God, but every time they tried to overreach and to achieve equality with God or to play God, it led to disaster.[20] In Psalm 8, the psalmist places humans somewhere between God and the animal kingdom. We rule over the lower creatures, but God rules over the entire universe. We are "little less than divine," but we are not divine. We must remember this lesson when approaching something as fraught with danger as enhancement or eugenic genetic engineering.

In conclusion, we are commanded to heal our fellow human beings, but we must not attempt to play God. Therefore, gene therapy is permitted and encouraged, but enhancement and eugenic genetic engineering are not in keeping with Jewish ethics and theology.

NOTES

1. See, for example, Fred Rosner, *Modern Medicine and Jewish Ethics,* second edition, Hoboken and New York, 1991, chapters 8, 9, 10 and 15.
2. W. French Anderson, *The Journal of Medicine and Philosophy* 10 (1985), pp. 275-276.
3. Anderson, pp. 276-83; Alan Emery and David Rimoin, eds., *Principles and Practice of Medical Genetics,* second edition, Edinburgh, 1990, pp. 2001-2010; Arthur and Elaine Mange, *Genetics: Human Aspects,* second edition, Sunderland, Mass., 1990, pp. 516-518; W. French Anderson, *Science* 256 (1992), pp. 808-813; A. Dusty Miller, *Nature* 357 (1992), pp. 455-460.

4. Anderson (1985), pp. 283-287; Emery and Rimoin, pp. 2003-2004; and Anderson (1992), p. 812 and note 36.
5. Anderson (1985) p. 287-288 and more recently in the same journal, 14 (1989), pp. 681-693 and in the *Hastings Center Report* 20 (1990), pp. 21-24.
6. Anderson (1985), p. 289 and see *Newsweek* (November 8, 1993), p. 47.
7. Dr. Marc Lappe in Elsie and Bertram Bandman, eds., *Bioethics and Human Rights*, Boston, 1978, p. 84.
8. Rabbi Walter Jacob, *Questions and Reform Jewish Answers: New American Reform Responsa*, New York, 1992, pp. 251-252.
9. Rabbi Azriel Rosenfeld, *Tradition* 13/2 (Fall 1972), pp. 71-74; Rabbi Seymour Siegel in Phillip Sigal, ed., *Bio-Medical Ethics: Three Theological Perspectives*, Grand Rapids, Michigan, 1984, pp. 10-11; Rabbi Lawrence Troster, *Reconstructionist* 49/6 (April-May 1984), p. 21; Rosner (above, note 1), pp. 188-189; Rabbi David Feldman, *Moment* 16/3 (June 1991), p. 4; Rabbi Walter Jacob (above, note 8) and Rabbi Abraham S. Abraham, *Nishmat Avraham*, vol. 4, Jerusalem, 5751, p. 217.
10. See *Sefer Hassidim*, ed. Reuven Margaliot, Jerusalem, 5717, p. 16, par. 22, and Rabbi Eliezer Waldenberg, *Tzitz Eliezer*, vol. 15, Jerusalem, 5743, no. 44.
11. See Rosner (above, note 1), Chapter 1; *Bava Kamma* 85a; *Midrash Shemuel* 4:1, ed. Buber, p. 54; Maimonides' commentary to *Mishnah Nedarim* 4:4; and *Shulhan Arukh, Yoreh Deah* 336:1.
12. This last point is made by Rosenfeld (above, note 9), p. 73, although I do not agree with the end of that paragraph.
13. See Genesis 30:37-39, *Berakhot* 20a, *Bava Batra* 110a and *Pesahim* 49a. Rosenfeld, pp. 73-74 and note 4, is the only one to note some of these sources and, as a result, he tends to permit genetic engineering.
14. Rabbis Troster and Feldman (above, note 9) and Rabbi Ari Burstein in an unpublished Hebrew responsum.
15. Cf. Rabbi Abraham Rabinowitz, *Tehumin* 2 (5741), pp. 509-510, who suggests enacting *takkanot* [rabbinic enactments] in order to control certain types of genetic engineering.
16. Anderson (above, note 5), repeatedly stresses this point.
17. See, for example, Kenneth Ludmerer, *Genetics and American Society*, Baltimore, 1972, and Daniel Kevles, *In the Name of Eugenics*, New York, 1985.
18. Hugh Gallagher, *By Trust Betrayed: Patients, Physicians and the License to Kill in the Third Reich*, New York, 1990.
19. See above, note 16.
20. Genesis 1:27; 3:5; 11:4; II Kings 18:28-19:37; Isaiah 14:3-20; Ezekiel 28:1-10.

THE KASHRUT OF VEAL RAISED ON FACTORY FARMS

EH 5:14 in *Rema*

Question: *Is it permissible for Jews to raise veal calves on factory farms? Is it permissible for Jews to purchase and eat veal raised on such farms?*

Responsum: In order to answer, we must first describe the way in which many veal calves are raised today. Here is one textbook description.

> The rearing system that has now come to be regarded as conventional operates as follows. Calves are transported from their farms of origin into large rearing units where they are placed in small, individual wooden crates about 150 cm long by 70 cm wide [60 x 28 inches], deprived of all access to bedding and solid food and fed twice daily regulated amounts of liquid diet similar in composition to conventional milk replacers except for iron content...
>
> Conventional veal crates... are only just big enough to contain a veal calf in the last weeks of its life. At this time the animal is unable to turn around, stretch its limbs, adopt all normal lying positions or groom itself. Deprivation of solid food denies the calves the opportunity to perform normal eating and rumination behavior...

They are kept this way until an age of 14 to 18 weeks, when they are taken to be slaughtered.[1]

Called "factory farming," this method of raising animals confines calves to crates in order to raise as many as possible in a short period of time using the fewest workers. The calves are fed an iron-free liquid diet which causes anemia and thereby satisfies the consumer demand for white or pale veal.

Given these facts, it is not surprising that Rabbi Moshe Feinstein (1895-1986), the most influential Orthodox authority in the United States, ruled in 1982 that it is forbidden for a Jew to raise veal calves in such a fashion.[2] He emphasized that those who do so are in clear violation of the prohibition of *tsa'ar ba'alei hayyim* [causing pain to animals][3] which, according to the Talmud,[4] is a biblical prohibition.

Granted, *tsa'ar ba'alei hayyim* is not an absolute principle. The Torah permits the slaughter of animals, providing every effort is made to limit their pain.[5] Rabbi Moshe Isserles, the *Rema* (d. 1572), allows one to pluck the wool from a sheep's neck prior to slaughter in order to facilitate proper *shehitah* [ritual slaughter] (*Yoreh Deah* 24:8). This is not gratuitous infliction of pain but a ritual necessity of the *shehitah* process. Similarly, "anything which is necessary to effect a cure [for human beings] or for other [similar] matters[6] does not constitute a violation of the principle of *tsa'ar ba'alei hayyim" (Even Haezer* 5:14). Many other authorities concur;[7] and this is the basis for allowing animal experimentation for the purpose of saving human lives.[8]

Thus the *halakhah* allows us to inflict pain on an animal if we have a good reason for doing so. Is the desire to produce whiter meat and attract more customers a good reason? Some might say yes,[9] but Rabbi Feinstein says no, since he views the entire enterprise as an attempt to deceive consumers into paying more money, which is forbidden by the Talmud.[10] Yet even if one were to claim that it is technically permitted to mistreat an animal for monetary reasons, Jews have always gone beyond the requirements of the law *(lifnim mishurat ha-din)* and refrained from hurting animals. As the *Rema* states at the end of the passage quoted above: "It is permitted to pluck feathers from live geese. . . *but Jews nonetheless refrain from doing so because it constitutes cruelty" (Even Haezer* 5:14).

Finally, in addition to being a violation of the prohibition of *tsa'ar ba'alei hayyim,* the practices described violate the letter or the spirit of a number of other laws regarding the treatment of animals.

1. It is forbidden to muzzle an ox when he treads out the corn (Deuteronomy 25:4). Veal calves are not treading corn, but it is cruel and inhumane to prevent them from nursing, drinking water and consuming the iron they require.

2. "Rabbi Elazar ha-Kappar ruled: One may not purchase a domestic or wild animal or a fowl unless one is able to feed it properly."[11] Veal calves are clearly not being fed properly.

3. The Torah states: "I will provide grass in the fields for your cattle; and you shall eat and be satisfied" (Deuteronomy 11:15). The Talmud derives from this verse that one may not sit down to eat until one's animals are fed.[12] If the rabbis were so concerned about the proper feeding of animals, they would never have tolerated the misfeeding of veal calves.

Thus far we have seen that it is forbidden for a Jew to raise veal calves in the fashion described. What about the Jewish consumer? Is he or she allowed to purchase and eat this type of veal? Our reply is once again in the negative.

First of all, as Rabbi Feinstein explains, because of the way they are raised, such calves are very weak and sickly which frequently leads to them being declared non-kosher. Stringent *shochtim* [ritual slaughterers] told him that only 15% of the calves are found to be kosher, while lenient slaughterers found 45% to be kosher. Thus, according to all *shochtim,* the majority of veal calves are not kosher and "pious people should not eat from such calves even if their intestines are checked".[13]

Secondly, a Jew who purchases veal might say: "The *stockman* is the culprit; *I* am not doing anything wrong. We would reply with the well-known halakhic principle: *"Ein mahzikin b'yedei ovrei averah"* – one may not aid and abet a transgressor.[14] By buying and eating veal raised in confinement, we encourage those who raise calves to continue these practices and imply that these practices are compatible with the humane tendency of *kashrut.* They are not.

Jews have always prided themselves that the Jewish method of slaughter is the most humane method possible. But one cannot divorce the moment of slaughter from the way in which the animal is treated before slaughter In recent years, there has been a growing trend among rabbis and *kashrut* supervisors to ensure that the animal's final moments are free from pain and trauma.[15] In accordancc with this, we must ensure that veal calves do not spend four to five months in inhumane and intolerable conditions. Jews should join the National Veal Boycott conducted by The Humane Farming Association, which has been very successful in forcing factory farms out of business.[16]

Finally, most of what has been said here also applies to geese and ducks which have been force-fed in order to enlarge their livers to produce *pâté de foie gras*. Such birds are forbidden both for reasons of *kashrut* (because they are often injured by the feeding process)[17] and because of *tsa'ar ba'alei hayyim*.

NOTES

1. John Webster, *Calf Husbandry, Health and Welfare*, London, 1984, pp. 175-178. Also see ibid., pp. 154-164, 178-186, and J. H. B. Roy, *The Calf*, fourth edition, London, 1980, pp. 75-79, 183-184, 276-281. For more up-to-date information, see note 16 below.
2. *Igrot Moshe, Even Haezer*, Part 4, Benei Berak, 1985, end of no. 92, pp. 164-165. Also see Rabbi A. Spero, *The Jewish Press*, Oct. 8, 1982, pp. 20 and 27; and Oct. 15, 1982, p. 19.
3. Regarding this principle, see the *Encyclopaedia Judaica*, Vol. 3, cols. 5-7; Noah Cohen, *Tsa'ar Ba'alei Hayim*, second edition, Jerusalem, 1976; and J. David Bleich, *Tradition* 22/1 (Spring 1986), pp. 1-36 = *Contemporary Halakhic Problems*, Vol. 3, New York, 1989, pp. 194-236. (The page numbers below refer to the second version.)
4. *Bava Metziah* 32b and *Shabbat* 128b. For the possible biblical sources of this prohibition, see Bleich, pp. 200-203.
5. Genesis 9:3-4 and Deuteronomy 12:15-16. On the limitation of pain, see Maimonides, *Guide of the Perplexed*, Part 3, chaps. 26 and 48 and *Sefer Hahinukh*, ed. Chavel, no. 440.
6. The word "similar" was added on the basis of the *Rema*'s source: *Issur V'heter Ha'arokh*, 59:36.
7. Bleich, pp. 217-224, 228-229.
8. Bleich, pp. 231-236.
9. See above, note 7, but also see Bleich, pp. 224-228, for those who would be opposed.
10. See *Bava Metzia* 60b.

11. Palestinian Talmud *Yevamot* 15:3, ed. Venice fol. 14d = *Ketubot* 4:8, fol. 29a.
12. *Berakhot* 40a = *Gittin* 62a and cf. Bleich, note 6.
13. Normally, only the lungs of an animal are checked. Rabbi Feinstein insists that the intestines be checked as well, but, even so, one should avoid eating veal.
14. *Mishnah Shevi'it* 5:9 = *Mishnah Gittin* 5:9. This principle refers to *Jewish* transgressors, but we have applied it to our case for the reason described.
15. Temple Grandin, *Judaism* 39/4 (Fall 1990), pp. 436-446; Phyllis Klasky Karas, *MOMENT* 16/1 (February 1991), pp. 40-45, 54-55. Also see the resolution of Conservative Rabbis in *Proceedings of the Rabbinical Assembly* 53 (1991), p. 215. For a recent debate on this topic, see *JTS Magazine* 9/2 (Winter 2000), pp. 10-11, 17. I agree with the views expressed there by Rabbi Arthur Lavinsky.
16. For information about factory farming and the National Veal Boycott, contact The Humane Farming Association, 1550 California Street, San Francisco, CA 94109.
17. See Rabbi Eliezer Waldenberg, *Tzitz Eliezer*, vol. 11, nos. 49, 55 and vol. 12, no. 52. For a brief description of how geese and ducks are force-fed, see Richard Schwartz, *Judaism and Vegetarianism*, Marblehead, Mass., 1988, p. 28. I was disturbed to see a recent article in *MOMENT* 25/3 (June 2000), pp. 39-41, extolling the "virtues" of *foie gras*.

IS IT A *MITZVAH* TO MAKE *ALIYAH*?

EH 75:3-4

Question: *Is it a mitzvah to make aliyah?*[1]

Responsum: The word *mitzvah* can mean good deed, but, technically, it refers to one of the 613 *mitzvot* or commandments in the Torah. This number was originally stated by Rabbi Simlai in the third century (*Makkot* 23b);[2] since then dozens of rabbis have enumerated the 613 commandments.[3]

As I have explained elsewhere,[4] *Eretz Yisrael* holds a unique place in Jewish tradition and history. As a result, we would expect our tradition to unanimously require *aliyah*. Yet, in fact, rabbinic literature contains at least five different approaches towards *aliyah*:

1. The early midrash of *Sifrei Devarim* (paragraph 80) relates that Rabbi Elazar ben Shamua and Rabbi Yohanan ha-Sandlar (ca. 150 c.e.) were on their way to study Torah outside of *Eretz Yisrael*. When they reached Sidon in Lebanon, they remembered *Eretz Yisrael*. They began to cry and they rent their garments and they recited the verse (Deuteronomy 11:31-32): "'When you have occupied it and are settled in it, take care to observe all of the laws. . .' Said they: 'Dwelling in *Eretz Yisrael* is equal to all of the other commandments in the Torah'. Whereupon they turned around and went back to *Eretz Yisrael*".

Nahmanides (1194-1270) followed their approach by ruling that it is a positive commandment to inherit the land and dwell therein.[5] Furthermore, he practiced what he preached, arriving in Jerusalem from Spain in 1267 and settling in Acre.[6] His opinion was accepted by a number of prominent medieval rabbis and is very popular among Israeli rabbis today.[7]

2. On the other hand, the above-mentioned Rabbi Simlai did not view *aliyah* as a *mitzvah* in and of itself but rather as a *makhshir mitzvah* or preparatory act which enables one to perform the *mitzvot* which can only be performed in Israel such as tithing and the Sabbatical and Jubilee years.[8]

> Rabbi Simlai expounded: Why did Moses our teacher yearn to enter the land of Israel? Did he want to eat of its fruits or satisfy himself from its bounty? But thus said Moses: "Many *mitzvot* were commanded to Israel which can only be fulfilled in *Eretz Yisrael*. I wish to enter the land so that they may all be fulfilled by me" (*Sotah* 14a).

Rabbi Simlai's approach was also followed by a number of medieval rabbis.[9]

3. Other talmudic sages did not rule explicitly on whether *aliyah* is a *mitzvah*, but tried to encourage *aliyah* and discourage emigration via specific legislation:[10] "Both husbands and wives may force their spouses to make *aliyah* (*Mishna Ketubot* 13:11). If a Jew wants to buy land in Israel, he may tell the non-Jewish owner to draw up the contract even on Shabbat (*Gittin* 8b and *Bava Kamma* 80b). "It is forbidden to leave *Eretz Yisrael* unless two *se'ah* (26.4 liters) of wheat sell for one *selah*. Rabbi Shimon said...if one can find any wheat at all, even if one *se'ah* costs a *selah*, he should not emigrate" (*Bava Batra* 91a).

Maimonides followed this approach. He codified the specific laws mentioned above,[11] yet he did not list *aliyah* as one of the 613 *mitzvot*. Indeed, Maimonides himself seems to have visited Israel in the year 1165, but did not remain.[12]

4. A number of medieval rabbis took a pragmatic approach. Rabbi Meir of Rothenburg (Germany ca. 1215-1293), for example, did not think that *aliyah* was one of the *mitzvot*, but he did think that whoever moves to Israel "for the sake of heaven and conducts himself in holiness and purity, there is no end to his reward, provided that he can support himself there".[13]

Rabbi Israel Isserlein (Austria, 1390-1460) ruled that it is certainly praiseworthy to live in Israel. However, since there is danger involved and since it is hard to earn a living there, "every person should judge his physical and monetary capabilities if he will be able to fear Heaven and observe *mitzvot* [in Israel]" (*Pesakim U'ketavim,* no. 88).

5. Lastly, there is the lone talmudic voice of the Babylonian sage Rabbi Judah who declared that whoever makes *aliyah* from Babylon to Israel actually *transgresses* a positive commandment (sic!).[14]

This negative approach to *aliyah* was followed by quite a few medieval rabbis.[15] Rabbi Judah the Pious (Ashkenaz, thirteenth century) ruled, for example, that it is preferable *not* to make *aliyah,* because he who does so will not be able to find a wife in Israel nor have time to study Torah due to the difficult economic conditions.[16]

In modern times, Rabbi Judah's approach has been adopted by the Satmar Hassidim who rabidly oppose mass *aliyah,* Zionism and the State of Israel due to their conviction that only God may redeem the Jewish people from Exile.[17]

Given these five approaches, it is difficult to state *the* halakhic approach to *aliyah,* since all five can be justified by talmudic and halakhic sources. Therefore, I would like to explain *my* halakhic approach to *aliyah.*

I made *aliyah* in 1972 because I believe that *aliyah* is both a *mitzvah* and a *makhshir mitzvah.* First of all, Nahmanides was right to list *aliyah* as a *mitzvah.* He remained in the minority only because all attempts to list the 613 *mitzvot* took place at a time when it was virtually impossible for most Jews to make *aliyah.* It seems that most rabbis saw no point in requiring something so dangerous and expensive that it was virtually unobtainable. By requiring *aliyah,* the rabbis would have turned almost the entire Jewish people into sinners.[18] But the thrust of Numbers 33:53 as well as of the entire Bible and Talmud is *that all Jews are supposed to live in Eretz Yisrael.* That is what God repeatedly promised our ancestors, that is why God redeemed us from Egypt, and that is where a large percentage of the *mitzvot* need to be observed.

Furthermore, *aliyah* is a *mitzvah* in the sense of a preparatory act because it enables one to perform not only the *mitzvot* connected to the land (no. 2 above) but *all* of the *mitzvot*. In Israel, one can observe Shabbat and all of the Jewish holidays with ease because the entire country is on "Jewish time". Israel is conducive to Torah study both in terms of vast opportunities and in terms of enabling the Bible and the Talmud to come to life. Living in Israel allows one to master Hebrew and thereby connect to our heritage which is written in Hebrew. Israel ensures "Jewish continuity" because, religious or secular, your children will most likely marry other Jews. Finally, Israel is the actualization of the prayers we have recited for 2,000 years: "May our eyes behold Your return to Zion with mercy"; "Blessed are you God who gathers the dispersed of Your people Israel".

In conclusion, one should make *aliyah* because living in Israel is a *mitzvah* in and of itself as well as a preparatory act which enables one to observe all of the *mitzvot* and to live a full Jewish life by living in a Jewish state.

NOTES

1. I.e. to immigrate to Israel. There is a vast literature on this subject. In English, see J. K. Mikliszanski, *Judaism* 12/2 (Spring 1963), pp. 131-141; J. David Bleich, *Contemporary Halakhic Problems*, vol. 1, New York and Hoboken, 1977, pp. 3-13: Ephraim Kanarfogel, *Jewish Quarterly Review* 76/3 (January 1986), pp. 191-215; Hershel Schachter in Shubert Spero and Yitzchak Pessin, eds. *Religious Zionism*, Jerusalem, 1989, pp. 190-212.
2. See Nahman Danzig, *Sinai* 83 (5738), pp. 153-158 for the history of this number.
3. See *Encyclopaedia Judaica*, vol. 5, cols. 760-783.
4. See my responsum in *Moment* 18/6 (December 1993), p. 34 = above, pp. 31-32. For the centrality of *Eretz Yisrael* in Jewish tradition, see above, p. 35, note 2.
5. Nahmanides to Numbers 33:53 and in his addenda to *Sefer Hamitzvot* by Maimonides, no. 4. Cf. above, p. 33 and notes 10-11, ibid.
6. Regarding Nahmanides' *aliyah*, see Rabbi Charles Chavel, *Ramban: His Life and Teachings*, New York, 1960, pp. 56-66.
7. *Responsa Ribash*, no. 101: *Responsa Tashbatz*, part 3, no. 288; Rabbi Ovadiah Yosef, *Torah Shebe'al Peh* 11 (5729), pp. 35-42; Rabbi Hayyim David Halevi,

Aseh Lekha Rav, part l, Tel Aviv, 5736, nos. 17-18. This was also the approach of Rabbi Abraham Isaac Kook which has been adopted by most religious Zionists in Israel.

8. For a good summary of the *mitzvot* dependent on the land, see Dayan I. Grunfeld, *The Jewish Dietary Laws,* vol. 2, London, Jerusalem and New York, 1972.
9. Rashbam to *Bava Batra* 91a, s.v. *ein yotzin* and Rabbi Baruch of Worms, *Sefer Haterumah,* Warsaw, 1897, p. 122a.
10. This legislation was probably a reaction to the dire economic situation after the Bar Kokhba revolt. See Gedaliah Alon, *The Jews in their Land in the Talmudic Age,* Jerusalem, 1984, pp. 659-661.
11. *Ishut* 13:20; *Avadim* 8:9-10; *Shabbat* 6:11; *Melakhim* 5:9-12; *Responsa of Maimonides,* ed. Blau, no. 365.
12. See *Encyclopaedia Judaica,* vol. 11, cols. 755-756. Regarding Maimonides' attitude towards *Eretz Yisrael,* see I. Twersky in Joel Kraemer, ed., *Perspectives on Maimonides,* Oxford, 1991, pp. 257-292.
13. *Responsa of the Maharam of Rothenberg,* ed. Berlin. Nos. 14-15, but cf. ibid. no. 79 where he states that making *aliyah* is indeed a *mitzvah.*
14. *Ketubot* 110b-111a. Space does not allow me to explain the involved Talmudic passage regarding "the three oaths" which follows.
15. See the exhaustive treatment by Aviezer Ravitzky, *Messianism, Zionism and Jewish Religious Radicalism,* Chicago, 1996, pp. 211-234.
16. See Kanarfogel (above, note 1), pp. 205-206.
17. For the Satmar approach, see Ravitzky, chapter 2 and *Encyclopaedia Judaica,* vol. 15, cols. 909-910.
18. Cf. *Bava Kamma* 79b and parallels: "one does not impose a decree on the public unless the majority can abide by it".

RESPONSA RELATED TO HOSHEN MISHPAT

THE ASSASSINATION OF PRIME MINISTER YITZHAK RABIN Z"L

HM 425 [1]

Question: *Yigal Amir, the murderer of Prime Minister Yitzhak Rabin z"l, justified his despicable deed by claiming that Rabin was a rodef (pursuer) and a moser (turncoat) who was about to hand over Jews or Jewish land to non-Jews.*[2] *Is there any halakhic justification for what Amir did?*

Responsum: Shakespeare once wrote that "The devil can cite Scripture for his purpose" *(The Merchant of Venice,* I, iii, 93); we now know that the devil can cite Talmud as well. Amir's interpretation is a gross distortion of Jewish law and tradition. What he did is murder, pure and simple, and entirely without legal justification.

There is nothing more sacred in the Jewish tradition than human life. As a rule, Jewish law posits that since God gave us life, only He has the right to take it away (Job 1:21; *Avodah Zarah* 18a). As a result, murder is forbidden. When Cain kills Abel, God is furious (Genesis 4:10): "What have you done? Your brother's blood cried out to me from the ground!". When Noah disembarks from the ark, God commands him the seven Noahide laws which include the prohibition of murder (Genesis 9:5-6). This prohibition is reiterated in the sixth Commandment which states (Exodus 20:13 and Deut. 5:17): "You shall not murder!" For the same reason, Judaism is opposed to suicide (*Genesis Rabbah* 34:13; Maimonides, Laws of Murder 2:2; *Sefer Hassidim*, ed. Margaliot, par. 675). Furthermore, there is the legal principle of *pikuah nefesh* which means that one is commanded to transgress almost every commandment in the Torah including the Sabbath, Yom Kippur and the dietary laws in order to save human life (*Yoma* 82a and parallels, 83a, 85a-b). Finally, the sacredness of every human life is encapsulated in the warning given to witnesses in capital cases: Why did God create all of mankind out of one single person? "To teach you that whoever destroys one life is considered as if he had destroyed the entire world, and whoever saves one life is considered as if he had saved the entire world" (*Mishnah Sanhedrin* 4:5).[3]

Thus, Judaism views human life as sacrosanct and only allows the taking of a life under four very special and unique circumstances. We shall now examine those circumstances and prove that by no stretch of the imagination can they apply to the case in question:

1. Capital punishment: The *Mishnah* allows capital punishment for a number of very specific crimes (*Mishnah Sanhedrin* 7:4, 9:1, 11:1). Relinquishing Israeli territory for the sake of peace is certainly not one of those crimes. Furthermore, only the *Sanhedrin*, or high court of Jewish law, may judge capital cases, and they stopped doing so around the year 30 c.e. (*Sanhedrin* 41a and parallels). Nonetheless, the sages of the Talmud continued to discuss capital punishment and to oppose it. Indeed, they added so many conditions that it would be almost impossible to execute a person:

> A *Sanhedrin* which kills once in seven years is considered murderous. Rabbi Elazar ben Azariah said: once in seventy years. Rabbi Akiva and Rabbi Tarfon said: if we had been in the *Sanhedrin*, no one would have ever been killed... (*Mishnah Makot* 1:10).

This assassination was obviously not based on the laws of capital punishment. Nonetheless, these laws teach us how reluctant the rabbis were to impose capital punishment even if it was preceded by due process of law.

2. Self-defense: The Rabbis ruled: "If someone is coming to kill you, rise early and kill him first" (*Sanhedrin* 72a and parallels). This principle, in turn, was based on the law of the intruder: "If a thief is seized while tunneling and he is beaten to death, there is no blood guilt in this case. If the sun has risen on him, there is blood guilt" (Exodus 22:1-2). Thus, it is permissible for a person to kill an

intruder at night lest the robbery lead to murder (*Sanhedrin* 72a and Maimonides, Laws of Theft 9:7-10). Clearly, these laws bear little resemblance to the case in question, but they establish the basic principle that one may only kill in self-defense when the act is carried out without premeditation and when one's own life is in imminent danger.

3. The law of the pursuer (*rodef*): We have learned in the *Mishnah* (*Sanhedrin* 8:7) that, if Reuven sees Shimon running after Levi in order to kill or rape that person, then Reuven may kill Shimon in order to prevent the crime. This law was explained at length by the Talmud and later codes of Jewish law.[4] Amir stated that Rabin was a "pursuer" who was poised to spill the blood of many Jews by giving up control over part of the West Bank and it was therefore permissible to murder him. This is a gross distortion of this law. First of all, the law of the pursuer only applies to a spontaneous act, whereas Yigal Amir planned this assassination for two years. Secondly, the law of the pursuer is only intended to save a potential victim from imminent death. There is absolutely no proof that withdrawing from certain territories will directly lead to the death of any Jews. On the contrary, Prime Minister Rabin, over half the members of the Knesset, and over half the population of Israel believe exactly the opposite – that it will save Jewish lives.

Lastly, this law does not refer to elected representatives, for if Yitzhak Rabin was really a pursuer, then so are all his followers and that would mean that Amir should have killed over half the population of Israel! In other words, even according to the law of the pursuer, this act was totally futile and senseless since the peace process will continue.

4. The law of the turncoat (*mosser*): A *mosser* is one who informs against his fellow Jews or hands over Jews or Jewish land to non-Jews. In the Middle Ages, Jews were often at the mercy of gentile rulers. When a Jew informed against his fellow Jew or handed him over to the authorities, this was considered a heinous crime because it frequently endangered not only the direct victim of the slander but the entire Jewish community. The Talmud records two cases where

an informer was killed by one of the Sages (*Berakhot* 58a and *Bava Kamma* 117a), and these stories were codified by Maimonides (Laws of Wounding 8:10). Yet this was the exception to the rule, as is made clear in Maimonides' code (ibid., 8:11). In actuality, Jews throughout the Middle Ages did not execute informers. In Germany they simply excommunicated them, while in Spain such an informer was judged by a court of rabbis who would pass sentence and hand the informer over to the gentile authorities for punishment.[5]

Amir compared Prime Minister Rabin to a turncoat who deserves death. This too is patently absurd. First of all, Prime Minister Rabin was not a turncoat; he was simply carrying out his job as the democratically elected Prime Minister of Israel trying to make peace with the Arabs. Secondly, the law of *moser* developed in the Diaspora when Jews were being ruled by gentiles, whereas Rabin was the sovereign, elected head of a Jewish State. Lastly, as mentioned above, Jews did not summarily execute turncoats without trial. Thus, this argument too falls by the wayside.

Until now we have simply reacted to Amir's twisting of the Jewish laws regarding murder. But the real tragedy is that Amir and his ilk have totally missed the entire point of religious Zionism, which views the State of Israel as the beginning of the redemption of the Jewish people. The democratic institutions of the State of Israel are not something to be "tolerated" outside of Jewish law. Rather, they are part and parcel of Jewish law – and living in accordance with its laws is as important as observing the Sabbath and keeping kosher. There are three ways of proving this assertion:

a) The Talmudic sage Samuel, who lived in third-century Babylonia, coined the phrase "the law of the land is the law" (*Nedarim* 28a and parallels), which meant that Jews must obey the laws of the countries in which they reside. But many rabbis state that this applies to a Jewish state as well.[6] If so, Jewish law requires Jews to observe the secular laws of the State of Israel.

b) Throughout Jewish history, every Jewish *kahal*, or community, was governed democratically on the basis of a passage in the

Talmud.[7] The State of Israel is the modern equivalent of the *kahal*, and its democratic institutions must be treated with the same respect and authority as the medieval *kahal*.

c) Rabbi Abraham Isaac Kook and Rabbi Shaul Yisraeli, two of the foremost religious Zionists of the twentieth century, have explained that, in our day, the democratically elected government and leaders of Israel have taken the place of the king and must be obeyed accordingly.[8]

Thus, not only did the assassin misread the Jewish laws of murder, but he totally misunderstood the significance of religious Zionism, which he supposedly represents.

How did this occur? How could religious Zionism which has done so much for the State of Israel spawn such a person? Rabbi Menahem Mendel of Kotzk once said that the Torah warns us not to turn God's commandments into idols.[9] Since the Six Day War, some religious Jews in Israel have turned their love of the Land of Israel into a form of idolatry which is used to justify all sorts of unethical behavior. When one commandment takes precedence over all others, it can lead to aberrations such as Baruch Goldstein and Yigal Amir. The dreadful actions of these two Jews must force the leaders of religious Zionism to search their souls and to overhaul their priorities and their educational system. The Land of Israel is very important, but so are a host of other Jewish values such as the value of human life, the State of Israel and the pursuit of peace. One commandment must not make us forget all of the others. I hope and pray that this will be a positive result of the terrible tragedy which has befallen us.

NOTES

1. This responsum was written on 3 Kislev 5756 as a spontaneous reaction to the Rabin assassination. My thanks to Rabbi Eliezer Diamond who critiqued the first draft. After appearing in *Moment*, it appeared in Hebrew in *Responsa of the Va'ad Halakhah of the Rabbinical Assembly of Israel* 6 (5755-5758), pp. 313-317.
2. The Washington Post, Nov. 12, 1995, pp. A1 and A30.

3. This is the correct reading of this *Mishnah* – see E.E. Urbach, *Tarbitz* 40 (5731), pp. 268-284 = idem., *Mei'olamam Shel Hakhamim*, Jerusalem 5748, pp. 561-577.
4. *Sanhedrin* 73ff.; Maimonides, Laws of Murder 1:6-16; *Shulhan Arukh, Hoshen Mishpat* 425.
5. *Encyclopaedia Judaica*, s.v. "Informers"; Maimonides, ibid.; *Shulhan Arukh, Hoshen Mishpat* 388:9 ff.
6. *Entziklopedia Talmudit*, vol. 7, cols. 307-308.
7. *Bava Batra* 8b. Regarding this passage, see Menachem Elon, *Jewish Law: History, Sources, Principles*, Philadelphia and Jerusalem, 1994, Chapter 19; Ephraim Kanarfogel, *Proceedings of the American Academy of Jewish Research* 58 (1992), pp. 71-106.
8. *Responsa Mishpat Kohen*, Jerusalem, 1984, no. 144, pp. 337-338, and *Amud Hayemini*, Tel Aviv, 1965, part I, nos. 7, 9.
9. Martin Buber, *Tales of the Hasidim*, vol. 2, New York, 1948, p. 279.

IS SMOKING PROHIBITED BY JEWISH LAW?[1]

HM 427

Question: *In light of dozens of scientific studies proving the dangers of smoking, is smoking prohibited by Jewish law? And if so, why is smoking so prevalent in the ultra-Orthodox community, which is so scrupulous about observing halakhah?*

Responsum: Since the Surgeon General's report first established the dangers of cigarette smoking in 1964,[2] more than forty responsa have been written on this subject.[3] The majority, whether Orthodox, Conservative or Reform, have ruled that cigarette smoking is prohibited by Jewish law, giving at least thirteen reasons for this conclusion. Six of the most cogent reasons follow.

1. Maimonides' *Mishneh Torah* contains a list of activities to be avoided for reasons of health *(De'ot* , Chapter 4). The introduction states:

> Seeing that keeping the body healthy and whole is the way of God, for it is impossible to understand or know anything about the Creator if one is sick, *therefore a person must distance himself from things which destroy the body and accustom himself to things which heal the body.*

Smoking is undoubtedly an activity "which destroys the body" and is therefore forbidden by Maimonides.

2. In Deuteronomy (4:9,15) God tells the Jewish people: "Take utmost care and watch yourself scrupulously". The Talmud *(Berakhot* 32b) derives from these verses that a person must scrupulously guard his physical health and this ruling was codified by Maimonides *(Rotzeah* 11:4) and the *Shulhan Arukh (Hoshen*

Mishpat 427:8). Thus, whoever smokes transgresses the commandment to "watch yourself scrupulously."

3. In addition to the general principle cited above, many specific activities were forbidden by the rabbis because they endanger human life, among them drinking water from an uncovered barrel lest a snake had poisoned the barrel with its venom *(Mishnah Terumot* 8:4-5), putting coins in one's mouth lest they transmit dangerous bacteria *(Yerushalmi* ibid. 8:3) and passing by a shaky wall or a rickety bridge lest they collapse (*Rosh Hashanah* 16b). Maimonides and the *Shulhan Arukh,* who codified these prohibitions, emphasize that these are merely *examples* and not an exhaustive list.[4] Thus, smoking is included in the list of things prohibited by our sages because they endanger human life.

4. According to the *Mishnah (Bava Kamma* 8:6), a person is not permitted to injure himself, a principle codified by the standard codes of Jewish law.[5] Smoking is a form of self-inflicted injury and is thereby prohibited by Jewish law.

5. The Talmud rules: *Hamira sakanta mei'issura* or "Regulations concerning danger to life are more stringent than ritual prohibitions" *(Hullin* 10a). In other words, in case of a possible transgression of ritual law, we rule in the direction of leniency, but in cases of possible physical danger, we rule in the direction of stringency. And thus the Rema rules in our connection (*Yoreh De'ah* 116:5): "And one should also be wary of all things which lead to danger because *hamira sakanta mei'issura* and one should worry more about a possible danger than about a possible ritual transgression". Therefore, even if one claims that cigarette smoking is not *necessarily* dangerous, since not all smokers die of cancer, it would still be forbidden on the grounds of doubtful danger.

6. Lastly, some smokers claim they have faith that God will protect them from the dangers of smoking. But the Talmud has already ruled on numerous occasions that one may not consciously place oneself in a dangerous situation because "one does not rely on miracles"[6] and this principle has also been codified in the *Shulhan*

Arukh in our context *(Yoreh De'ah* 116:5). Thus, a smoker may not rely on miracles and is required to stop smoking.

If smoking is so clearly prohibited by Jewish law, why is it still so prevalent in ultra-Orthodox circles? This may be because a number of ultra-Orthodox *poskim* [rabbinic authorities], while admitting that smoking is not a good idea or discouraging the practice, have consistently refused to prohibit smoking. The most prominent among them was Rabbi Moshe Feinstein (1895-1986), who wrote five responsa on the subject.[7] Ordinarily, the Talmud discourages one from disagreeing with a prominent rabbi after his death since he cannot defend himself (*Gittin* 83b), but smoking is no ordinary issue. It is an issue of *pikuah nefesh,* or the saving of a life, which takes precedence over almost all of the *mitzvot* in the Torah *(Sanhedrin* 74a). Furthermore, it is essential to refute his approach because he has had a greater influence on the ultra-Orthodox community than any other halakhic authority.

1. In 1964, Rabbi Feinstein refused to prohibit smoking "in particular because a number of great Torah sages in past generations and in our own smoke". This is, of course, irrelevant. First of all, those sages did not know that smoking was dangerous. On the contrary, they thought it was beneficial and healthful.[8] Indeed, when R. Israel Meir Hakohen, the *Hafetz Hayyim* (1838-1933), heard from doctors that smoking was dangerous for "weak people", he ruled that they should stop smoking![9] Secondly, Rabbi Feinstein believed that great Torah sages have *da'at Torah* [the Torah view] which is influenced by *ruah hakodesh* [God's holy spirit] and are therefore infallible.[10] Yet these beliefs were invented in modern times and are entirely foreign to normative Judaism.[11]

2. Furthermore, Rabbi Feinstein seemed totally unaware of the scientific facts about the dangers of smoking. Even in his 1981 responsum, he compares smoking to "many types of food which people enjoy very much like fatty meat and very strong food". On the other hand, halakhic authorities who studied the scientific evidence ruled that smoking is absolutely forbidden by Jewish law.[12]

3. The Talmud says that it is dangerous to circumcise a child or let blood on a cloudy day or on a day when the south wind blows, but since many have trodden on that path [and not been harmed] "God protects the simple" (Psalms 116:6) *(Yevamot* 72a). Rabbi Feinstein and others extend this principle to the case of smoking. Since many have smoked and not died, "God protects the simple." This analogy, however, is very questionable. "God protects the simple" may apply when the public is "simple" and unaware of the dangers involved, but today every smoker has been warned innumerable times of the dangers of smoking and yet ignores the warnings. Therefore, he is not "simple" and God does not protect him. Rather, the smoker is consciously placing himself in danger, which is clearly forbidden.

Furthermore, in the five cases where the Talmud invokes this principle,[13] the activity itself is innocuous (e.g., eating) or a *mitzvah* (e.g., circumcision) and the rabbis were willing to ignore some *external* danger by invoking the principle of "God protects the simple." But smoking *itself* is lethal and the principle is therefore not relevant.

Lastly, a number of rabbis stress that the Talmud only invokes this principle when the danger involved has not been proven, but it cannot be utilized when we can clearly see that smoking *is* dangerous and that God does *not* wish to protect the smoker.

4. In addition, Rabbi Feinstein's approach to cigarette smoking is clearly contradicted by his approach to marijuana smoking. In a little-known responsum from 1973 concerning marijuana, he stated: "It is obviously forbidden by a number of basic laws in the Torah. *First of all, it damages and destroys the body".* The inconsistency is glaring. Marijuana is forbidden because it destroys the body, a fact that remains to be proven, while smoking, which is clearly deadly, is permitted according to the principle that "God protects the simple"! He continues: "Furthermore, marijuana causes a great craving which is greater than the craving for food and the like which are essential to sustain human life". And cigarettes do not? (Indeed, Rabbi Feinstein himself makes a similar statement about cigarettes in his 1981 responsum.) Lastly, in his responsum on marijuana, he states: "It is certainly forbidden to bring oneself to a craving greater than

that for food and for a thing which a person has no need for". Are cigarettes inherently different? If marijuana is forbidden because it destroys the body, arouses a great craving and serves no purpose, then cigarettes should be forbidden for the very same reasons!

5. Lastly, many people assume that Rabbi Feinstein and others refused to forbid smoking because of the Talmudic principle, "one should not impose a restriction on the community unless the majority can abide by it" (*Bava Kamma* 79b and parallels). In other words, we cannot prohibit smoking because many smokers will not be able to abide by our decision. However, none of the responsa on smoking invoke this principle. Second, most people are non-smokers, so the majority can easily abide by this decision. Finally, this principle is irrelevant because, as we have seen, *this is not a new restriction*. Smoking is *already* forbidden by the existing *halakhah* and there is no need for any new restriction.

In conclusion, Rabbi Feinstein's position on smoking was one of the most unfortunate halakhic decisions of our generation. If he had forbidden smoking in 1964, thousands of Jews who looked to him for halakhic guidance would have kicked this deadly habit. Who knows how many lives might have been saved? But it is not too late. We hope that the ultra-Orthodox *poskim* will soon realize what all other *poskim* realized years ago: Smoking is lethal and is therefore forbidden by Jewish law.[14]

NOTES

1. This responsum is an abbreviation of a Hebrew responsum which appeared in the *Responsa of the Va'ad Halakhah of the Rabbinical Assembly of Israel* 4 (5750-5752), pp. 37-52.
2. According to the Surgeon General's Report of 1990: "Smoking related illnesses cause more than one of every six deaths in the United States" (*Washington Post*, September 26, 1990, p. A4). In Israel, smoking causes 6,000 deaths every year – *over ten times the road accident toll* (*The Jerusalem Post*, April 30, 1999, p. A5).
3. See my Hebrew responsum, pp. 50-52, for an extensive bibliography. For English responsa see: Rabbi Moses Aberbach, *Tradition* 10/3 (Spring 1969), pp. 49-60; Rabbis J. David Bleich, Solomon Freehof, and Seymour Siegel in Elliot Dorff and Arthur Rosett, eds., *A Living Tree*, Albany, 1988, pp. 345-

359; R. Nathan Drazin in Leo Landman, ed. *Judaism and Drugs,* second edition, New York, 1973, pp. 71-81; Dr. Fred Rosner, *Modern Medicine and Jewish Ethics,* second edition, Hoboken and New York, 1991, pp. 391-403.

4. *Rotzeah* 12:6; *Hoshen Mishpat* 427:10; *Yoreh Deah* 116:5.
5. Maimonides, *Hovel Umazik* 5:1; *Shulhan Arukh, Hoshen Mishpat* 420:31.
6. *Megilah* 7b, *Pesahim* 50b, *Kiddushin* 39b, *Shabbat* 32a, *Ta'anit* 20b and see *Zohar* to *Bereishit* 111b.
7. *Igrot Moshe, Yoreh Deah,* Part 2, no. 49 (from 1964); *Yoreh Deah,* Part 3, no. 35 (1973); *Hoshen Mishpat,* Part 2, no. 76 (1981); *Noam* 24 (1982), pp. 302-308; and *Pe'er Tahat Efer,* Jerusalem, 1988, p. 19. All quotes below are from these responsa.
8. See, for example, the responsa cited by R. Freehof (above, note 3), pp. 354-355.
9. *Likutei Amarim,* 1967, no. 13.
10. See R. Moshe Feinstein, *Igrot Moshe, Yoreh De'ah,* Part 2, p. 6. Also see Alan Yuter, *Judaism* 28/2 (Spring 1979), pp. 155-159; Lawrence Kaplan in Moshe Sokol, ed., *Rabbinic Authority and Personal Autonomy,* Northvale, N.J., 1992, pp. 1-60; Gershon Bacon, *The Politics of Tradition: Agudat Yisrael in Poland,* 1916-1939, Jerusalem, 1996, pp. 47-57.
11. See Kaplan, Bacon and R. Hayyim David Halevi, *Aseh Lekha Rav,* Vol. 2, Tel Aviv, 1978, pp. 146-147.
12. See, for example, R. Hayyim David Halevi, *Aseh Lekha Rav,* in nine different responsa; R. Eliezer Waldenberg, *Tzitz Eliezer,* Vol. 15, no. 39.
13. The concept also appears in *Shabbat* 129b; *Niddah* 31a; *Avodah Zarah* 30b and *Yevamot* 12b.
14. For many years, Rabbi Ovadia Yosef, the leading sefardic *posek* in Israel, refused to forbid smoking. In recent years, he changed his mind. See *Yedi'ot Aharonot,* May 27, 1997, p. 8.

ORIGINAL PLACE OF PUBLICATION OF THE ARTICLES IN MOMENT MAGAZINE

Why do Jews Sway when They Pray?, August 1993, pp. 18, 70

Returning Territories for the Sake of Peace, December 1993, pp. 34, 89

Institutionalizing Parents with Alzheimer's Disease, April 1991, pp. 22-23, 42

Torah Study vs. Earning a Living, June 1992, pp. 24-25, 64

Investigating the Charities to which We Contribute, February 1992, pp. 17-18

Telling the Truth to Terminal Patients, October 1992, pp. 22-23

Genetic Engineering, August 1994, pp. 28-29, 67

The *Kashrut* of Veal Raised on Factory Farms, February 1993, pp. 26-27, 86

Is it a *Mitzvah* to Make *Aliyah*?, February 1995, pp. 28-29

The Assassination of Prime Minister Yitzhak Rabin z"l, February 1996 pp. 24-25

Is Smoking Prohibited by Jewish Law?, October 1991, pp. 14-15

GLOSSARY OF HEBREW TERMS

beraita – a teaching of the *Tanna'im* [early sages] not included in the *Mishnah.* There are thousands of *beraitot* in the Babylonian and Palestinian talmuds and in other rabbinic works.

Eretz Yisrael – the Land of Israel

gemara – the commentary of the *Amoraim* (ca. 200-500) on the *Mishnah,* also known as the Talmud

halakhah (adjective: *halakhic*) – Jewish law

midrash, (plural: *midrashim*) – both rabbinic exegesis of a specific verse and the books containing such exegesis

Mishnah – the basic book of the Oral Law which was edited by Rabbi Judah the Prince ca. 200 c.e.

mitzvah (plural: *mitzvot*) – one of the 613 commandments in the Torah; also: a good deed

posek – halakhic authority

pikuah nefesh – saving a human life, which sets aside almost all of the *mitzvot* in the Torah

Shulhan Arukh – one of the most widely-accepted codes of Jewish law written by the sefardic Rabbi Yosef Karo (1488-1575) with ashkenazic glosses by Rabbi Moshe Isserles, the Rema (1525-1572)

tzedakah – the *mitzvah* of giving money, food and clothing to the poor

yeshivah – an academy for Talmud study

SUBJECT INDEX